Protecting the child
an HVA guide to practice and procedures

Copyright © Health visitors' association, 1994

published by
Health visitors' association
50 Southwark Street
London SE1 1UN

designed by
Peter Brawne

page make-up by
Quest, London EC1

printed by
College Hill Press, London SE1

cover photograph by John Birdsall
library photo posed by models

ISBN   1 872278 18 3

Contents

Foreword [6]
Introduction [8]

1 The context [11]
2 The health visitor and community nurse's role [17]
3 Identifying children at risk [23]
4 Assessment and referral [39]
5 Child protection procedures [45]
6 Court orders and care proceedings [57]
7 Court proceedings [63]
8 Records and record-keeping [67]
9 Accountability [74]
10 Prevention [78]

Conclusion [84]
References [85]
Appendices
1 Child protection plan agreement [88]
2 Child summary sheet [91]
3 Child protection summary sheet [92]

Foreword

The past two decades have seen increasing attention paid to the issues of child abuse – physical and emotional and, more recently, sexual – and to the statutory protection of children. There has also been a growing awareness of the need to understand more fully the individuals who abuse.

In the 1960s, when the issue of child abuse first began to be recognised by the health, social and legal professions, it was thought to be rare, and was seen very much as an individual, isolated problem; the actions of perpetrators were seen as the product of mental illness.

Today child abuse is seen clearly for what it is: neither rare nor isolated, and very much a product of our social and political environment, and of society's attitudes to children and to women – for the victims of sexual abuse in particular are most often female. Protecting children at risk of abuse continues to be a grave public and professional concern.

Research and analysis of reports of inquiries into child abuse have given us a far greater understanding of how we may identify, prevent and deal with it more effectively. But there remains much to learn. The sad fact is that, ultimately, no outsider can prevent abuse occurring; professionals can only be alert to its possibility and do all in their power to intervene before lasting damage occurs.

The Children Act 1989, implemented in 1991, resulted from this greater understanding and awareness; as do its powers, which enshrine the fundamental principles: that the child's interests and welfare must always come first, and that agencies must, wherever possible, work in partnership with children and parents.

The Act also underlines the need for agencies and professionals to work together to protect the child; for better understanding and communication between the various professionals concerned, so that mistakes highlighted by many of these widely publicised inquiry reports are not repeated. These are principles which should inform all community, family and child care practice.

Child protection, in its formal sense, comprises a relatively small part of most community nurses' workloads, but can absorb a disproportionately large amount of time, energy and personal investment. This needs recognition.

But the taboo that often surrounds child abuse brings with it fears that may, needlessly, hamper the work of professionals seeking to work in the best interests of the child.

The aim of this book is to explain, in simple language and logical progression, how the formal child protection procedures work and what makes good practice in child protection. Its main readership is likely to be health visitors and school nurses, since they are more centrally involved than their primary health care nursing colleagues. But it will be of interest and relevance to all nurses and others working with children and families in the community.

It is, I believe, an immensely helpful source of information and clarification. It will, I hope, form a useful contribution to all our efforts to protect those who most need and deserve our help: our children.

Margaret A Buttigieg
Director, Health visitors' association

Introduction

Protecting children is about working together: professionals working with parents and other family members; professionals working with each other, across disciplines and agencies; agencies working together across the statutory and voluntary sectors.

Above all, child protection is about working with children.

But child protection is not solely the responsibility of the professionals and statutory authorities; it is the responsibility of society as a whole to ensure the safety of its children and that they have health, education and the opportunity to live to their full potential.

The interests of children must come first, by law. This is the fundamental principle underlying the Children Act 1989; a principle with which all statutory and voluntary agencies involved in child protection are explicitly expected to comply. The Act states that the child's wishes must be heard when decisions are made about their future, and that parental responsibility for the child rests – and remains unless the child is legally adopted – with its natural parents. It requires all professionals to work with parents and children in the child's best interests.

The nursing profession plays an important role in child protection; specifically in the identification and referral to the statutory authorities of children at risk of or suffering abuse. Health visitors and school nurses in particular, because of their daily contact with children and families and their specialist training and expertise in preventive health care, have a key role in supporting vulnerable families and children, helping parents care adequately for their child and ensuring that everything possible is done to avert situations where a child might come to harm. But all members of the nursing profession who work with families and children in the community have a very important role in the identification and referral of children at risk, and in assisting in the child protection process.

The work of health visitors and school nurses often continues when other statutory agencies have formally withdrawn: in providing ongoing support for those families to whom – for whatever social, environmental or personal reasons – bringing up a child does not come easily. Practice nurses too, within the framework of the family health services and working with other members of the primary health care team, are in a position to develop relationships with families, to identify indications of possible abuse or factors leading to abuse, and to refer children and their families to the appropriate authorities and services.

This guide has been written for all nurses working with children and families in the community. It is specifically aimed at those community nurses most likely to be involved in child protection: health visitors and school nurses. But it will also be of use to the many other nurses employed in the community and the primary health care services who have regular contact with young children and their families in the course of their work, such as practice nurses, community paediatric nurses and midwives.* Nursery nurses and health visitor assistants will also find it of use to explain the child protection process.

The aim of the guidance is to clarify the role and responsibilities of the community nurse; the support you can expect and demand from your managers and nurse advisers; the roles of health authorities, NHS trusts and GPs, social services departments and other statutory agencies such as the police; the role of the non-statutory services such as the NSPCC, and the legal and policy frameworks which determine local child protection procedures and practice. The guidance also covers the statutory powers embodied in the Children Act 1989, its various orders and how to use them, and other important legal issues such as court orders and procedures, accountability, confidentiality and record-keeping.

Every registered nurse working with children and their families will, at some point, have known the anxiety and responsibil-

---

* Unless otherwise specified, the generic term 'community nurse' will be used throughout to describe all registered nursing professionals working with children and families in the community setting.

ity of suspecting child abuse and the difficult decision of whether to make a referral to the statutory child protection authorities. You will know the frustration and distress when a referral is not acted on. Community nurses often work in isolation, with limited access to peer group support and clinical supervision. You often take important and far-reaching decisions based on your professional judgement alone. This guidance does not replace the professional support and training which should be available to you. All community nurses should be given training in national and local child protection policies and procedures. This guide aims to help to allay some of the common concerns and fears about child protection work and to suggest ways in which health visitors, school nurses and all nurses working in the community can ensure that you work with fellow professionals in the best interests of the children and families you seek to support and protect.

HVA child protection working party

Andrew Andrews
health service adviser, Nabarro Nathan solicitors

Sue Botes RGN RHV
professional officer, Health visitors' association

Jill Clemerson RGN RSCN RHV
clinical nurse specialist, child protection
City and East London Family and Community Services

Catherine Jackson
journalist, Health visitors' association

Sue Sefi RGN NDN RHV MA
child protection adviser, Oxford Community NHS Trust

June Thompson RGN RHV
freelance medical journalist

1 The context

1.1 Current trends in child abuse

Recorded incidence of child abuse rose steadily from 1975, when local authorities first started keeping registers of children at risk of or suffering deliberate abuse. Typical of this trend are the figures for the period 1989-1991: in March 1989 there were 41,200 children whose names were entered on local authority child protection registers in England. By March 1990 this had risen to 43,900, of whom 26,800 were new entries. A year later, in March 1991, these figures had risen to 45,300 and 28,200 respectively. A reversal in this overall upward trend then began, apparently, to occur: in March 1992 a fall in the numbers of children on local authority registers was recorded: to 38,600; and again there was a fall, to 32,500 in the year to March 1993.[1]

However, this change should be seen in the context of the removal, in April 1991, of one of the most commonly-used categories for registration: that of 'grave concern'. This category was used to describe those children whose situation did not meet any of the other, more exact categories, but who were assessed as likely to be at significant risk of harm and therefore in need of protection. 'Grave concern' was also used to bring onto the register children whose siblings, or other children in the same household, were known to have been harmed or where the household included a known abuser. Numbers of children registered under this category fell from 21,100 in 1991 to just 2,700 in 1993 – and the figures will continue progressively to fall as these children are either removed from the register or re-allocated to another category. However, numbers of children registered under the remaining categories continue to rise: from 24,200 in 1991 to 29,700 in 1993. The percentage of children registered under neglect rose from 20 per cent of the total in 1992 to 26 per cent in 1993; physical injury from 28 per cent to 37 per cent; sexual abuse from 17 per cent to 26 per cent, and emotional abuse from seven to 11 per cent. New registrations remained more or less the same (24,700 in 1993: some 29.6 children per 10,000 under the age of 18).

Throughout the years in which the registers have been maintained, children in large families and those with young parents have tended to be over-represented on local authority registers.[2] Debt and unemployment have been shown to contribute significantly to family stress, with consequent impact on the children,[3] and family stress itself is widely recognised as a contributing factor to child abuse.[4]

Unemployment, debt, homelessness and family breakdown are unlikely to disappear from twentieth century society; families will continue to face serious financial, material and personal and relationship difficulties. These factors are likely to continue to be reflected in the incidence of child abuse.

Downward pressure on social security benefits and reductions in qualified staffing levels in health and social services are also likely to impact on the ability of professionals to intervene and, most importantly, to provide support to vulnerable families, to prevent the occurrence of abuse.

There is also evidence[5] that fragmentation of both health and education services following the NHS and Community Care Act 1990 and the Education Reform Act 1988 is damaging to effective communication and liaison between the various agencies involved in identifying and protecting children at risk. This must be of serious concern, since department of health policy on child protection rightly puts the highest premium on the importance of inter-agency working and effective communication and co-ordination between the many services and professionals involved.[6]

1.2 The Children Act 1989

The introduction, in 1991, of the Children Act 1989 enshrined in law new principles and a new, unified framework for the care and protection of children.

The decision to review all child care legislation came from growing concern about the complexity of child care law. The

Children Act 1989 brings together under a single piece of legislation both private (relating to family disputes) and public (relating to interventions by the statutory authorities) law and introduced a new local magistrate's court, the family proceedings court, to hear the majority of cases concerning the care and well-being of children. Urgent and more complex cases continue to be heard in the county or high court.

The Act's other main area of legislative change relates to the provision of services to children by local statutory and voluntary agencies and the responsibilities of local authorities for the inspection and registration of child-care premises.[7]

1.2.1 **The principles**

The Children Act 1989 is in twelve parts. Of chief concern to community nurses are:[7]

- part one, outlining the principles of the Act
- part two, concerning custody and contact orders in family proceedings
- part three, covering local authority responsibilities towards children in need
- part four, on the care and supervision of children where this responsibility is shared between the parents and local authority
- part five, covering emergency protection of children
- part ten, covering local authority provision and registration of child-minding and day care.

The legal framework of the Children Act 1989 rests on eight fundamental principles:

- the child's welfare always comes first
- children with disabilities have the same rights as all children; their needs as children should always come first
- parents continue to have responsibility for the child, unless the child is adopted
- children should, as far as possible, be brought up within their own families
- professionals should consult and work in partnership with children and parents
- the views of the child and parents should be taken into account

when decisions are made about a child's future
- a child's religious beliefs, racial origin, culture and language should be taken into account when decisions are made about their future
- court orders should be used only as a final resort.

1.2.2 **Parental responsibility**

Parental responsibility is defined under the Act as 'all the rights, duties, powers, responsibility and authority which, by law, a parent has in relation to a child and his property'. Parental responsibility is held by both parents if they were or are married to each other at or subsequent to the child's conception; if unmarried, the mother alone holds parental responsibility, but the unmarried father can either agree parental responsibility with the mother or seek to obtain it by a court order. Guardians, or other individuals appointed by a court, can also share parental responsibility with the parent(s), as will the local authority social services department where a care order has been made. In such situations the social services authorities are given powers to set limits on the parents' access to the child and will have final say in decisions about the child's future.

The Children Act 1989 stresses that parental responsibility must remain with the child's parents wherever possible. Parents retain sole or shared parental responsibility for their child unless and until the child is adopted. Statutory services will only be given powers to share parental responsibility where it can be proved to a magistrate or judge that the child is either:
- suffering or likely to suffer significant harm, and
- the harm or likelihood of harm is due to
   a) failure, or likelihood of failure by the parents to provide a 'reasonable' level of care to their child, or
   b) the child is beyond the parents' control.

Parents who fail to provide a 'reasonable' standard of care will not automatically be held at fault: the Act acknowledges that a child may be unwilling to accept their care. They are, however, expected to seek help. If they do not seek help, this may in itself be interpreted as failure to provide reasonable care.

1.2.3 **Children in need**

The Children Act 1989 requires local authorities to provide services to children defined under the Act to be 'in need'. This should not be confused with a child's exposure to 'significant harm', which relates to social services intervention in cases of child abuse.

This is a critical distinction and of particular importance to health visitors and school nurses because it relates directly to your particular contribution to child protection: primary preventive health care.[8]

Under the Act a child is deemed 'in need' where it is believed that without the provision of services by a local authority:

- she is unlikely to achieve and maintain, or have the opportunity to achieve and maintain a reasonable standard of health and development, or
- her health and development is likely to be significantly impaired, or where
- she is disabled.

'Development' includes physical, intellectual, emotional, social and behavioural development; 'health' includes both physical and mental health. 'Disabilities' include loss or absence of sight, hearing and ability to speak, mental disorder and 'substantial and permanent handicap' through either illness, injury or congenital defect, and 'such other disability as may be prescribed'.[7]

Local authorities are required to take 'reasonable steps':

- to identify the numbers of children 'in need' within their geographical area
- to provide services to prevent children in the area suffering neglect or ill-treatment
- to publish information about local services available for children 'in need'
- to ensure this information is available to families who might benefit from such services
- to maintain a register of children with disabilities.

Health visitors and school nurses in particular, through your close and regular contacts with children and families and knowledge of local environments and circumstances, are uniquely placed to contribute to local authorities' collection of data on children 'in need'. Caseload, school and community health profiles are an invaluable source of information for local authorities when planning and providing services to support vulnerable families.

Every local authority should have an agreed definition of 'need', drawn up in consultation with health and other statutory and voluntary agencies. All community nurses should be informed of this definition, and of how to contribute to the collection of data on levels of 'need' among children and their families. Managers of community nursing services should ensure that these data are collected, and used, where necessary, to argue for more resources or for changes in resource allocation.

'Need' should not be used simply to describe children with special health or medical conditions; interpreted more broadly, it may include circumstances such as homelessness and access to public services: health care, education, welfare support and advice and transport.[8] Local authority assessments of need can in this way provide a useful mechanism for highlighting social and environmental factors which adversely affect families' ability to care adequately for their children. This enables both health and local authorities to intervene more effectively with families known to be vulnerable and so avoid crises and the need for emergency intervention by the statutory authorities.

The range of services required to be made available by local authorities include:

- day care, including child-minders
- out-of-school and holiday schemes
- family centres and family support projects
- benefits and welfare rights advice.[7]

Social services departments are also responsible for providing training and support to childminders and for the inspection and registration of all day care services, including local authority nurseries, playgroups and private childminders.[7]

These services all play an important role in primary and secondary preventive care of families under stress where children may be at risk of harm or neglect.

2 The health visitor and community nurse's role

The role of the health visitor or nurse is to observe, assess, record and refer. It is not her responsibility to diagnose, nor to investigate child abuse.

Of the various community nursing disciplines, health visitors and school nurses are most likely to be involved in formal child protection procedures.[6] However, every community nurse working with children and their families should be vigilant to the possibility of abuse and familiar with the procedures for making referrals to the appropriate statutory authorities.

Social services, the police and the NSPCC are the only agencies with statutory powers to investigate suspected and actual child abuse, and health authorities and NHS trusts are required by the Children Act 1989 to work with them in the protection of children.[6]

For the health visitor and school nurse in particular, this will mean assisting in:

- the prevention of abuse and neglect
- the identification and assessment of children causing concern, and
- the referral for investigation of children who are at risk of or subject to abuse or neglect.

2.1 The child protection adviser

Every NHS trust and health authority unit employing health visitors, school nurses and other nurses working with children in the community is expected to ensure that field staff have access to a senior nurse manager with specific responsibility for co-ordinating child protection work. (Trusts and units providing midwifery services are expected to designate a senior midwife with similar responsibilities.[9])

The majority of community nursing units have appointed a specialist child protection adviser. This designated senior nurse or child protection adviser must be a qualified health visitor.[9] Her role is to co-ordinate child protection work between the community nursing unit and social services and the other local agencies concerned. Her remit includes:

- monitoring child protection procedures and practice within the trust
- ensuring local child protection policies and procedures are known and understood by health visiting and community nursing staff
- providing clinical leadership and supervision to field staff
- assessing and arranging training and updating for staff, including induction training for newly-appointed staff
- providing support and advice to field staff involved in the child protection process
- attending child protection conferences where necessary or where requested
- putting in place procedures for the rapid transfer of records when a family moves to another area
- providing an overview of child protection issues and incidence across the area covered by the unit.

Every health visitor, school nurse and community nurse should know how and where to contact in an emergency her child protection adviser or designated senior nurse.

2.2 The health visitor

The health visitor is widely recognised as the community nurse with key responsibility for child protection.[7,9]

Families with whom the statutory child protection authorities are involved generally form a relatively small proportion of the health visitor's caseload. But involvement with these families can create a disproportionate amount of work and absorb a considerable amount of time and energy. Involvement in a case where a child has been abused can also be extremely stressful and distressing for the health visitor concerned, no matter how experienced.

The role of the health visitor is to observe, assess, record and refer. It is not her responsibility to diagnose nor to investigate child abuse.[9]

The health visitor's prime responsibility is for child health surveillance. She sees every mother and new-born child at home, following discharge from hospital. She will continue to monitor the child's health and well-being, in partnership with the GP and primary health care team, until the child is five. Her continued contact with the child and family means she is in a position to assess the child's physical and mental well-being and development, in both the long and short term. Her ongoing relationship with the child and family also allows a more informed assessment of their situation, and the degree of risk to which the child may be exposed.

The health visitor is specifically trained in the identification of mental and physical deviation from normal child development and behaviour. Her additional training in social policy and social aspects of ill-health means her assessment of the child's well-being will extend beyond the parameters of physiological and medical symptoms to include wider social and environmental factors.[10]

The health visitor has a key preventive role. Her skills and training, and her access to the child and family, mean she is in a position to identify factors which may indicate a family vulnerable to child abuse. She can then agree with the family a care plan which will help the parents provide more appropriate care for their child.

The health visitor is also accepted by clients.[11] Health visitors, unlike social workers and the police, have no statutory powers to enter the home of a member of the public, nor to remove a child believed to be at risk. Her health remit and the universality of the service means that a visit from the health visitor may be seen as a welcome source of support, without the social stigma of, say, a visit from a social worker. Most other health and social services professionals visit families only when asked to do so, or in response to a specific referral.

Health visitors also have links with local support networks and sources of information and help, as well as with the other community health care services and members of the primary health care team. This enables her to draw from a broad range of local resources and agencies to give help and advice to vulnerable families and to contribute to the provision of ongoing support for these families.

2.3 **The school nurse**
School nurses are central to the ongoing monitoring and care of children's health from school entry at age five to when the child leaves school at 16 or 18.

School nurses provide a vital link between the health and education services, taking health promotion into the classroom and identifying health problems that may prevent a child getting the maximum benefit from his education. Like the health visitor, the school nurse will also have ongoing contact with the child's family. While she may not have a permanent base on a school premises, she is a key member of the school community.

All school nurses are registered general nurses, but they will not all have received further training prior to practice in the community. School nurses without the necessary skills and qualifications should not attempt to take on child protection responsibilities; nor should they be required to do so.[9]

A reliable system of handover from the health visitor to the school nurse is vital to ensure continuity of care. Any concerns about a child must be included in the records passed from the health visitor to school nurse.[9] In some cases the health visitor will maintain involvement with the child and family beyond the age of school entry: where, for example, there are already concerns for the child or the child has particular health needs.

The school nurse needs to be familiar with both the local authority and local education authority (or school) child protection procedures. She will also need to be aware of the children in her schools whose names are entered on a child protection register. It is the responsibility of the school nurse manager or child protection adviser to ensure systems are in place to collect and collate this information so that it is readily available to community nursing staff who need to know.[9]

It is not the role of the school nurse to investigate suspected incidence of child abuse. However she is an important part of the chain of referral. Every school must have a designated member of staff with responsibility for child protection. Where a school nurse suspects a child may be experiencing abuse, she will contact this designated teacher, or the school's head teacher, who will alert the appropriate social services officials. Teaching staff may seek her professional advice and assessment of the child and family situation when considering whether to make a referral to social services.

The school nurse, like the health visitor, has an important role in preventive health care, and in strategies to identify and protect children before abuse occurs. She has unique access to the school-age child through regular health surveillance checks. She is seen as 'outside' the education system and this, combined with her health remit, often makes her a more acceptable source of advice and support to school children. Many school nurses run regular drop-in sessions where they offer advice and counselling to older children on a one-to-one basis.

Some school nurses have training in family planning and help run clinics specifically aimed at younger people, where they are likely to be in a position to identify sexual abuse of older children. School nurses will also work closely with families to help them tackle particular problems of, say, enuresis or eating disorders.

In class, school nurses work with teaching staff on health promotion and health education projects, including sex education and sexual health. They often run specific health promotion events focusing on particular issues, such as smoking, alcohol and drug abuse and other issues of concern to the children within their schools. All these activities form part of the process of helping the school-age child achieve her maximum personal, health and educational potential.

2.4 The practice nurse

The practice nurse is, in common with her health visitor and school nurse colleagues, in a key position to observe and identify children at risk of or experiencing abuse. However she is unlikely to have ongoing participation in the formal child protection process.

It is important that practice nurses are familiar with the wider context in which they work with children. But it is not part of her remit to attempt to manage a situation of suspected or actual child abuse or neglect; nor should she be required to do so. Her role – as is the case for all nursing professionals – is to identify and refer, not to intervene. If she is concerned about a child's well-being, and abuse is suspected, she will immediately inform the child's GP and, if appropriate, health visitor. In an emergency she will contact social services, in line with agreed local procedures.

However practice nurses do have a major role in identifying children at risk of harm. They are often the first contact for children and families attending the GP surgery for regular check-ups or medical advice and treatment. The practice nurse may have responsibility for aspects of the child health surveillance programme, and for immunisations. She may also be responsible for health screening programmes, and for specific health promotion programmes aimed at school-age children. Again, her health remit will make her a trusted and accepted source of advice and support, and the child or parents may disclose to her information which gives her reason to be concerned about the child's well-being.

All practice nurses should receive training in local child protection procedures. General practitioners and FHSA nurse advisers should ensure that practice nurses' training needs are assessed regularly and that appropriate training, including joint training with other agencies, is provided, and that staff are released by their employing GP to attend courses.

3 Identifying children at risk

The welfare of the child must always come first. Fears of jeopardising your relationship with the parents should not be allowed to influence your professional judgement at the expense of a child's safety.

Health visitors, school nurses and community nurses have a key role in bringing to the attention of the statutory social services children who are at risk of harm or neglect. Your role is to identify, record and refer; it is not your role, nor that of any member of the medical profession, to investigate suspected or reported incidents of child abuse. You should immediately refer any child you believe to be at risk either to your local social services or, if this is for any reason not possible, to the police or NSPCC, all of which have statutory powers to intervene.

3.1 Assessing risk

A number of factors have been identified which may guide your assessment of the extent to which a child is at risk of harm. These should be used with caution, however;[12] no two situations are the same, and rigid application of a check-list of indicators may lead to children being either missed or wrongly identified as at risk of harm. Nor should it be assumed that families with indicating factors are unable to function adequately without professional intervention. However, used in conjunction with your professional assessment of the child, family and their circumstances, these factors may help you identify a potentially vulnerable family or child and be used to justify particular vigilance and the provision of additional support and resources.

It is equally dangerous to attempt to predict or identify a potential abuser. This could give rise to stereotyping, and racial, gender, class or cultural bias. Health visitors and nurses working with children in the community should aim to work also with the parents, building on their abilities and strengths. To label a parent as 'abusive' goes against this basic principle of partnership; it could even become a self-fulfilling prophecy if it led to your withdrawal of positive support and encouragement, or to your treating a parent or carer with suspicion.

However the welfare of the child must always come first.[8] Fears of jeopardising your relationship with the parents should not be allowed to influence your professional judgement at the expense of the child's safety and well-being.

All health visitors, school nurses and nurses working with children and families in the community should receive training and updating in the identification of signs of child abuse, both in their foundation preparation on child protection and through local, inter-agency training programmes. FHSAs should ensure that such training is available to practice nurses and that GPs release practice staff to attend.

3.2 Identification

The 1991 department of health study of reports of official child abuse inquiries from the years 1980-1989[13] offers useful insight into the difficulties of accurately predicting or identifying situations where a child may be at risk of or suffering harm. The findings of the inquiries show that abuse – physical, emotional and sexual – is usually triggered by a unique and, by its very nature, unpredictable combination of events or circumstances. However the study is useful in that it highlights blocks which in retrospect were seen to have prevented professionals responding appropriately to signs of child abuse. These include:

1. the unknown – the professional lacked expertise and training in identifying signs/symptoms of abuse
2. the known but not acknowledged – the professional failed to distinguish between accidental and non-accidental injury; distrusted or dismissed an information source; failed to take perceived signs seriously
3. misinterpreted/decoy data – the professional incorrectly interpreted the situation, signs or signals; was led to focus on one sign or aspect so that their attention was diverted from another

4 competing tasks – the professional was under pressure from other demands
5 fragmented picture – agencies failed to co-ordinate information
6 no record – information was deliberately withheld from the professional; professionals failed to record information because it was seen as outside their remit or role
7 individual bias – professional was not able to remain objective about information; the professional confused fact and opinion
8 mistaken certainty – the professional placed too much emphasis on one information source or point of view; jumped to conclusions based on first assumptions
9 stereotypings and prejudice – the professional's personal beliefs or prejudices were allowed to cloud their ability to assess the situation correctly.

The study also revealed a number of critical signals which professionals mistakenly ignored:

- warnings from neighbours and friends
- warnings from other family members
- warnings from the parents
- statements from the children themselves;

and highlighted a number of other risk factors, including:

- parents' resistance to professional intervention
- parents' abrupt behaviour change
- parents deceiving professionals
- parents showing violence towards professionals
- loss of contact with a family through:
  - child's failure to attend day nursery or school
  - parents' refusal to allow access to the child
  - family moving home.

3.2.1 **Warning signs**

No professional is infallible. Crises of confidence, loss of objectivity or inability to cope with situations can occur at any stage in a health visitor or nurse's career, particularly when working under stress. Professional and peer group support is vital. If you suspect a child may be at risk of or experiencing harm but are uncertain whether to make a referral, you should discuss the case with an experienced colleague or with your child protection adviser or designated senior nurse. Practice nurses will find it helpful to share their concerns with the child's health visitor and the family's GP.

Ability to acknowledge doubts and to ask for help from colleagues and senior staff are professional strengths, not signs of weakness or failure. As will be explained later in greater detail (see p. 68), sharing information with colleagues within the community nursing or primary health care team is not a breach of confidence when it is done in the best interests of the child.

3.2.2 **Physical abuse and neglect**

The department of health study of child abuse inquiry reports[13] identifies the following common factors in families where a child has been abused:

- parental history of unstable, damaging or violent adult relationships
- parental violence outside the family
- parental history of violence to children
- deaths of other children within family.

Another study of prevention of child abuse and neglect[14] identifies the following factors as common to families where there is a high risk of physical child abuse and neglect:

Parents
- abused or neglected as a child
- aged 20 years or less at birth of first child
- single parent or separated / divorced
- partner not biological parent
- abuse of alcohol, drugs
- history of violent behaviour, suicide attempts
- poor education
- mother pregnant or with chronic health problem

Family
- history of abuse, neglect or deprivation
- socially isolated
- moves home frequently or poor housing
- poverty: parent(s) unemployed or low-waged

Child
- previously abused or neglected
- under five years of age
- premature or low birth weight
- currently underweight
- birth defect or chronic health problem
- delayed development
- prolonged period of separation from mother
- cries frequently and difficult to comfort
- feeding difficulties
- adopted, fostered or step-child.

A third study[12] identifies the following as factors suggesting a family may be more vulnerable to child abuse and neglect:

Parents
- unhappy childhood: rejection, childhood separation, emotional cruelty, rigid discipline, physical abuse
- early parenthood: may lead to unrealistic expectations of child, unmet dependency demands on child
- psychological problems: stress at time of abuse; depression, anxiety; attempted suicide
- bereavement: post-natal death of previous child
- drug and alcohol abuse
- ill health
- poor marital/partner relationship
- social problems, including tension within extended family, debt, social isolation
- poor quality social support.

Child
- born too soon: parents not emotionally ready for child; child premature, low birth weight, more prone to illness
- born sick or with disability: abnormal pregnancy, abnormal labour or delivery; neonatal separation or other separations in first six months; illness in first year; mother's illness in first year; feeding difficulties
- born different: child does not conform to parents' expectations
- born unwanted: child not wanted in first place; seen as poor substitute for death of other, more valued person.

3.2.3 **Sexual abuse**
Children of all ages, boys and girls, can be subjected to sexual abuse, often by adults within their family or close family circle. Many kinds of sexual abuse, such as masturbation, fondling and oral sex, leave no lasting physical evidence. However children who are sexually abused can suffer physical injury, such as damage to the genitals and anus.[15,16]

Children and young people of all ages will often show their emotional distress through their behaviour: through disruptive behaviour and 'acting out', sexualized behaviour, compulsive behaviour or behaviour disturbances such as bed-wetting and disturbed sleep, as well as depression and poor self-esteem.[17,18]

However these external signs may be less evident among older children and young people, who tend to be more adept at concealing their feelings.[19]

Health visitors and community nurses may find the following checklist and action programme a useful reference if they suspect a child may be suffering sexual abuse:[20]

Age 0-5 Monitor
regression / hostile or aggressive behaviour

Refer for investigation
bath or bed-time fears / failure to thrive / depression / over-reaction to certain adults / nightmares / chronic urinary tract infections / soreness of genitals or bottom

Investigative interview with child
visible bruising or bleeding of the genitals / venereal disease / inappropriate sexual play or knowledge / simulation of sex act / compulsive masturbation / use of sexual language / disclosure.

Age 5-12 Monitor
reluctance to go home / sudden mood changes / tummy aches / regression / problems with peers / aggression / regression / psychosomatic conditions / disruptive in class / sudden access to unusual amounts of money

Refer for investigation
running away / poor school attendance / reluctance to discuss family / eating disorder / low self-esteem / self-neglect / general fearfulness / obsessional washing / social isolation / reluctance to go to bed / highly emotional behaviour

Investigative interview with child
pregnancy / disclosure / venereal disease / genital injury / sexual behaviour / self-exposure / sexual drawings or stories / compulsive masturbation / sexual promiscuity / alcohol abuse / substance abuse.

Age 12+   **Monitor**
delinquency / psychosomatic conditions / school problems / peer problems / authority problems / delayed sexual development

Refer for investigation
eating disorder / depression / menstrual problems / self-mutilation / alcohol abuse / drug abuse / sexual boasting / sexualised behaviour

Investigative interview with child
prostitution / sexual promiscuity / pregnancy (under 14) / disclosure / injury to genitals / venereal disease (under 14) / self mutilation / sexual assault.

The role of the health visitor and community nurse will not extend beyond initial identification of concern and subsequent referral. But it is important not to act in any way that may place the child in danger, or may interfere with any possible criminal prosecution. It is therefore vital that all health visitors, school nurses and community nurses working with children should be trained in local inter-agency procedures for handling incidents of suspected or actual sexual abuse. Joint training with the police and other professionals will help ensure that you understand your own and one another's roles and responsibilities, and that errors are not made which leave a child at continued risk of harm.

3.2.4 Physical examinations

No health visitor or nurse should ever attempt to examine a child beyond your usual remit, such as child health surveillance checks. Full physical examinations should only be carried out by a registered medical practitioner, with the consent of the child or those holding parental responsibility for the child. The consent of the child must be obtained if she is able to understand the implications of the situation, and specifically if she is over the age of 16.

Children should not be subjected to repeated, intrusive, painful and distressing medical investigations. Any practitioner attempting to give a child a physical examination without either the child's or parents' consent, or without a court order, may risk prosecution for assault under civil law.[7]

3.3 Case studies

Neglect 1

Rob and Jenny, one-year old Laura's parents, are both under 20. They have recently moved into a rented maisonette. Laura has been seen twice in A&E in the past six weeks, both times with bruising to her head and shoulders. She is admitted to hospital after the second attendance. Her parents say she fell downstairs.

The family's health visitor has visited Rob and Jane on both occasions, having been notified of Laura's attendance at A&E. She recommends that they carry out urgent repairs to the stairway where, according to Rob, Laura slipped through missing bannisters. Jane, however, separately tells the health visitor that she is now the only bread-winner and has to leave Laura with Rob when she goes to work, but that she thinks Rob is too rough with the child.

The health visitor visits Rob and Jenny again while Laura is still in hospital and finds the repairs have not been done. She is concerned that Rob and Jane appear not to be taking seriously the risk to Laura's well-being. She refers the case to the local social services department and a child protection conference is held. The conference decides that Laura's name should be entered on the child protection register under the category of 'neglect', on grounds that she has suffered significant harm as a result of her parents' poor supervision and unsafe conditions in the home.

Neglect 2
Jeanette has two young children: one of 18 months and the other of just eight months. When she brings them to clinic the health visitor on duty notes that the baby weighs considerably less than he should and that he looks emaciated and miserable. When asked, Jeanette says he is difficult to feed and keeps vomiting. The older child appears fit and well.

The health visitor is concerned and refers the baby to the GP at the clinic, who immediately refers him to hospital, where he is admitted.

Medical investigations reveal no organic reason for the baby's weight loss and poor feeding. He gains weight rapidly during his six-week admission. The paediatrician diagnoses non-organic failure to thrive.

The baby is subsequently placed on the child protection register under the category of neglect, on grounds that he has suffered significant harm through Jeanette's failure to feed him adequately and the conference believes there is no guarantee this will not continue on his discharge from hospital.

Failure to thrive 1
Ten-month old Ben is admitted to hospital for investigations after progressively losing weight since weaning at four months. His mother says she is feeding him an adequate diet, but the health visitor has been concerned about the amount of solids he has been getting.

The health visitor has been monitoring Ben's weight at the fortnightly clinic and at eight months, when his weight has dropped to its six-month level, she refers him to the GP.

The GP continues to see the mother and baby for a month and Ben gains a little weight. The mother reports to the GP that Ben's stools are 'smelly and yellow' and the GP decides to refer the child to the consultant paediatrician for tests. Following admission to hospital three weeks later, Ben's failure to thrive is confirmed as coeliac disease.

Failure to thrive 2
Alex brings her baby, Susie, to clinic regularly. She is an anxious parent, constantly in need of reassurance and support from her health visitor. Twice she has taken Susie to A&E in the middle of the night, saying she will not feed. Alex tells the health visitor feeding is a constant problem, but when the health visitor sees mother and child at home Susie is feeding eagerly.

Susie is not gaining weight, however, and the health visitor refers her to the GP. Arrangements are made to admit her to hospital for tests.

Alex goes with Susie to the hospital and continues to care for her there, including making up her feeds. Susie still fails to gain weight, although the tests reveal no organic reason for her failure to thrive. Finally arrangements are made to video Alex feeding Susie, and the feeds are tested for strength.

It is discovered that Alex is making up consistently under-strength feeds and removing the bottle from the baby during feeds, preventing Susie from taking in enough nourishment. Alex is diagnosed as suffering from Munchausen's syndrome by proxy and referred for treatment at the mother and baby unit on the hospital psychiatric ward.

Physical abuse 1
Jasmine's father brings her to clinic for her eight-month hearing test. The health visitor notices bruises on Jasmine's inner arm and around her neck. When she comments on the bruises the father says he is concerned about them too. The health visitor knows that he and Jasmine's mother are separated and that the mother has main custody of the child. Jasmine's father says he thinks the baby is left with a lot of different child-minders.

The health visitor decides to refer Jasmine to social services and asks the GP to examine her. The GP makes an immediate referral to the hospital paediatrician and, following a skeletal survey, a fractured clavicle is found and the baby is immediately admitted to hospital.

A child protection conference is called at the hospital and Jasmine's name is placed on the register under the category of 'physical abuse' as she has suffered significant harm and the conference believes she is at risk of further abuse.

Physical abuse 2
Eight-year-old John comes to the school nurse's room because, he says, his back hurts. He has no clear explanation, but finally says he fell off his bed the previous night.

The school nurse is suspicious. John often comes to see her with minor health complaints; she knows he does not get on with his step father and John has said his step father hits him occasionally. On this occasion the school nurse decides to report her concerns to the head teacher, who has responsibility for child protection in the school.

The head teacher contacts John's mother at work, to ask her to collect John, who is clearly in pain. John's mother says she can't leave work. The head teacher then contacts the local authority senior education social worker, who immediately contacts social services.

John is interviewed by a social worker the following day. The social worker also arranges for him to be examined by a clinical medical officer, and John's mother is asked to attend. John's mother says the bruises found on his lower back were caused when he fell off a table, messing about with his brother. John says nothing during the medical examination.

The school nurse contacts the family's health visitor, who says she has no concern about the care of the two other, younger children in the family. The social worker decides to call a child protection conference, where the school nurse raises her long-standing concern about John's well-being, as evidenced by his poor appearance and frequent, minor ailments, as well as repeated incidents of more severe injury. John's name is entered on the register as the case conference agrees he is at risk of 'significant harm'.

Sexual abuse

Four-year old Louise tells her best friend Leroy at play-group that her daddy kisses her 'pee pee'. Her friend tells his mother, who informs the play group leader. The play group leader remembers an incident a few weeks earlier when another child, who had been playing with Louise in the wendy house, came to her saying that Louise was 'pulling down her knickers'.

The play group leader refers the case to social services, and a planning meeting is held. The meeting agrees to interview Louise's father, and to video an interview with Louise with her mother present. At the interview, attended by a social worker and a member of the police child protection team, Louise repeats what she said to Leroy. However her mother refuses to agree to a police forensic medical examination.

A child protection conference is held and Louise's name placed on the register under the category of sexual abuse. The conference believes she has probably been sexually abused and fears that her mother is not able to protect her.

Emotional abuse

Linda has four children, aged between 12 and three. Linda herself was brought up in care and a number of foster homes.

The local health visitors know her well and have been involved with all four children. Linda has a reputation for contacting the health and social services regularly in times of crisis but rarely attending follow-up appointments or referrals. On at least three occasions in the past 12 years she is known to have gone abroad for periods of up to six months, leaving the children with family members or friends, and not always together.

When Linda fails to bring her youngest, Tracey, for her three-year surveillance check, the health visitor decides to visit the family at home. Linda's 16-year old sister is there, with Tracey, but says Linda has gone abroad 'for a month'. Tracey says her mum has gone 'for always' and that her aunt says 'mum doesn't love you any more'. The health visitor contacts the school nurse at the local primary school attended by the other children. The school nurse reports that the other children are all staying with different family members and friends and don't seem to know where their mother is or when she is due back.

The health visitor refers all four children to social services and a child protection conference is called. The conference decides to register all four children's names. The conference agrees that Linda's inconsistency of care and lack of contact with and apparent abandonment of the children amounts to emotional abuse.

3.4 **Children with disabilities**

Common myths and assumptions about disability and child sexual abuse include:[21]

- people don't abuse disabled children
- sexual abuse is less harmful to disabled children
- you can't prevent the abuse of disabled children, so it's not worth trying
- disabled children are more likely to make false allegations of abuse
- if a disabled child has been abused, it's best to leave well alone.

Children with disabilities may be particularly vulnerable to abuse. Abuse may also cause lasting physical or mental harm, leading to permanent disability.

Low birth weight and disabled children may be at risk because their special health, educational and care needs put more stress emotionally and financially on their parent(s).[2,12,14]

Parents struggling to cope with these additional demands may also be struggling with confused feelings of anger, denial and guilt: internal and external conflicts which may themselves contribute to abuse occurring.

Studies carried out by the NSPCC have revealed a number of factors which have contributed to the failure of professionals to identify and act on suspected cases of abuse of children with disabilities.[22,23] These include:

- social values: the myth that abuse of children with disabilities causes them less harm than able-bodied children; professionals are therefore less likely to intervene

- child's situation: children with disabilities may be isolated from social and family contact; are often more dependent than their non-disabled peers
- nature of the disability: child may have difficulty in telling about abuse because of communication disabilities or because the child lacks confidence
- denial: professionals may be reluctant to believe that disabled children are vulnerable to abuse.

Given the additional problems experienced by the child and possible blocks to communication, professionals need to be particularly vigilant to:
- disclosure by the child
- emotional, behavioural or physical signs
- contact with a known or suspected abuser
- reports by third party.[23]

Health visitors, school nurses and community nurses working with children with severe disabilities should be particularly aware that:
- spontaneous disclosures of abuse are likely to be rare
- where a child does try to tell, communication difficulties and denial by adults may prevent the message getting through
- signs of abuse may be less obvious or visible.

Information given by other children should always be taken seriously.[22] Where a child with disabilities has been abused or is believed to be at risk of abuse, the same principles and procedures for their protection and intervention by statutory agencies apply. If you suspect that a child with disabilities is, or is at risk of, being abused, you should follow the usual steps for assessment and referral as you would for any child, in accordance with local policies and procedures.

3.5 Female genital mutilation

Female genital mutilation refers to the cultural practice of female circumcision: the excision or infibulation of parts of female genitalia. Female circumcision is practised in a number of countries, mainly located across central Africa. Infibulation is practised in Sudan, Somalia, Senegal and Mali; circumcision is practised by some groups in Nigeria, Kenya, Ethiopia, Mauritania and also the republic of Yemen and Oman.[24] It is essentially a cultural, not religious, practice.

People whose cultures include the practice and who are now resident in the UK may wish to continue to circumcise their daughters. It is a strongly-rooted tradition, regarded as beneficial to the girl, who would otherwise be seen as unmarriageable.

Under the Prohibition of Female Circumcision Act 1985, female genital mutilation is illegal in this country except on specific physical and mental health grounds. However young girls continue to be at risk. Registered doctors or traditional health workers may still perform illegal genital mutilation of young girls in the UK. Alternatively their families may send them on a visit to their country of origin or one where circumcision is legally permitted.

Pre-pubescent girls of seven to ten are most at risk; school nurses in particular will need to be vigilant with girls of this age. You should be alert to indications that the girl is expecting to leave the country for a period, to an abrupt and unexplained absence from school, and to clues and signals from the girl herself. Similarly, health visitors may be in contact with a family with younger children where the older girl is reaching the at-risk age.

Statutory intervention must be handled with great care and sensitivity if the practice is not to be driven underground and the family and community alienated. Education and raising awareness among young girls and women are key to preventing its continuation. Advice from the campaign groups concerned is that female genital mutilation should not be labelled as child abuse, but that professionals should be clear that it is abusive. It is illegal, however, as stated above, and local authorities may intervene, under section 47 of the Children Act 1989, on grounds that the child is at risk of harm. Legal proceedings can be taken to prevent the child being removed from the country or to ensure that health and social services authorities have access to her. A girl at risk of genital mutilation may be placed on the child protection register under the category of physical abuse. Removal from home should be considered only as a last resort.

A girl already subjected to genital mutilation should not be placed on the child protection register; she is unlikely to be at further risk of harm in this particular respect. But she should be offered counselling and medical help. It may also be appropriate and acceptable to provide her with contacts for local support groups.

Health visitors, school nurses and other nurses working in areas whose populations include the at-risk cultural groups should receive training in how to handle situations where you suspect a girl may be at risk of genital mutilation.

As with any case of suspected child abuse, girls believed to be at risk should be referred to social services. Local authorities in those areas with significant numbers of people from communities known to practise female genital mutilation should have agreed inter-agency procedures for protecting girls at risk of harm. A member of the ethnic group concerned should always be included to advise investigations.

The sensitivity of this issue cannot be stressed too highly. Help must be offered both to girls at risk and to older girls and women who have been circumcised, but it is vital that health care and medical professionals act only in consultation with advisers from the communities concerned.

Further information on female genital mutilation can be obtained from:

Forward
The Africa Centre
38 King Street
London WC2E 8JT
℡ 071 379 6889

London Black Women's Health Action Project
Community Centre
38 Cornwall Avenue
London E2 0HW
℡ 081 980 3503

4 Assessment and referral

No professional, however experienced, can prevent abuse occurring. But where a child is at risk, your vigilance and prompt referral may prevent her coming to more serious, long-term emotional or physical harm.

Where you suspect a child may be at risk of, or subject to, neglect or harm, your first decision will be whether the situation requires emergency intervention. Your first step, therefore, will be to assess and decide the extent of the risk or harm to which the child is exposed.

It is important to gain as full a picture as possible of the child and family's circumstances and background before taking any action, to act calmly, and to weigh every decision carefully before taking any action.

If a young child is visibly harmed, you may find it useful to record the position and extent of the bruises or other injuries on a body map diagram.

It will help to discuss the child's situation with an experienced colleague, with your child protection adviser or, in the case of practice nurses, the child's GP and health visitor.

It is also good practice to raise your concerns with the child's parents before taking any action, unless sexual abuse is suspected.

In cases of child sexual abuse, by revealing your concerns to the parents you may inadvertently alert the perpetrator. This may not only put at risk the safety of the child but may jeopardise any police investigations into the situation and possible criminal proceedings.

You should follow local policy and procedures on how to proceed and to whom to refer if you suspect a child is being sexually abused.[7]

In all cases of actual or suspected emotional, physical or sexual abuse, you should assess child's immediate situation:
- is it an emergency?
- is the child in need of immediate protection?
- does the child need urgent medical attention?

If yes:
- immediately contact the social services, police or NSPCC
- record details of incident and actions taken
- inform the parents of your concerns and of any actions taken (unless it would be inappropriate or unsafe to do so)
- inform other professionals who have contact with the child/family
- inform your child protection adviser.

If no:
- discuss your concerns with the parents
- check child's medical/health visitor records for any previous problems/concerns
- consider precisely what is causing you concern
- talk to colleagues who have had contact with the family
- talk to GP, child protection adviser, manager or other experienced colleague
- decide whether to refer to social services, in consultation with child protection adviser or senior nurse manager
- record in full details of incident and actions taken
- inform other professionals who have contact with the child/family.

4.1 **Referral**

Social services are the lead agency with responsibility for child protection.[6] They are officially responsible for investigating all child protection referrals and co-ordinating the inter-agency response. Only social services officers, police officers and NSPCC officers have statutory powers to intervene and to remove children from a parent's care.

All health visitors, school nurses and nurses working with children in the community and likely to be involved in child protection should be trained in and familiar with local policies

Figure 1: Child protection referral

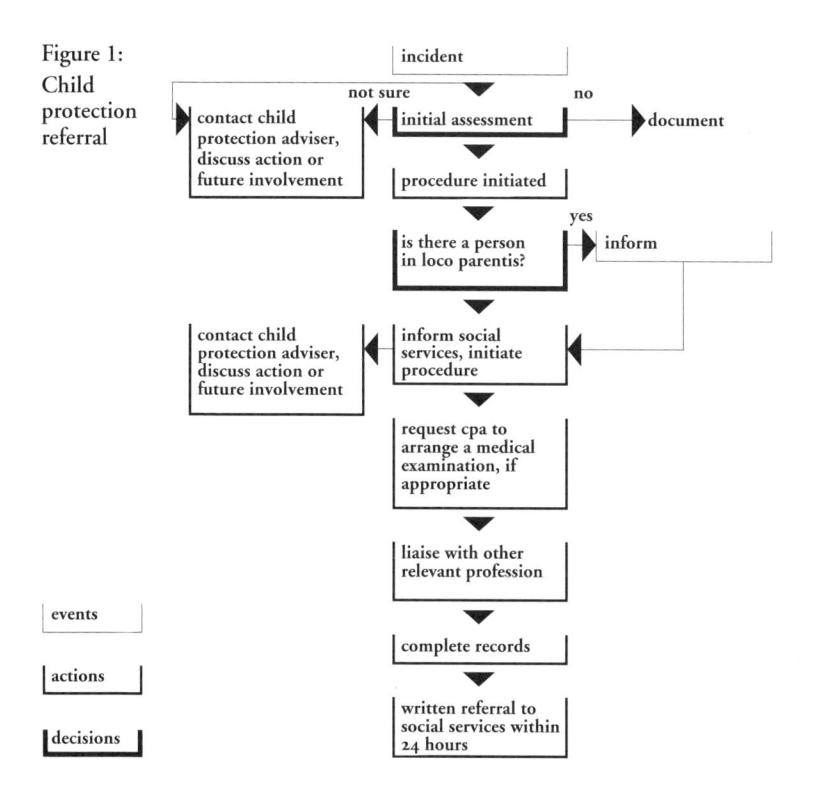

```
                              incident
                                 ▼
              not sure                        no
contact child  ◄──── initial assessment ────► document
protection adviser,
discuss action or
future involvement
                                 │
                                 ▼
                       procedure initiated
                                 │
                                 ▼                yes
                       is there a person ──────► inform
                       in loco parentis?
                                 │
                                 ▼
contact child  ◄──── inform social ◄─────────────┘
protection adviser,   services, initiate
discuss action or     procedure
future involvement
                                 │
                                 ▼
                       request cpa to
                       arrange a medical
                       examination, if
                       appropriate
                                 │
                                 ▼
                       liaise with other
                       relevant profession
                                 │
                                 ▼
                       complete records
                                 │
                                 ▼
                       written referral to
                       social services within
                       24 hours
```

| events |
| actions |
| decisions |

and procedures for the protection of children. You should know whom to contact in an emergency, and you should be provided with a copy of the local area child protection committee (ACPC) handbook on child protection procedures. Health visitors and community nurses working for NHS trusts or health authorities should also have a copy of your employer's guidelines on the specific procedures which are the responsibility of the local community health services. Practice nurses should know how and where to refer children you believe to be at risk of harm.

The local social services department is the first point of referral for health visitors and community nurses concerned about a child's safety or well-being. It may help to discuss these concerns first with your child protection adviser, an experienced colleague or the family's GP.

When making a referral to social services:

- make sure you speak directly to a social worker, and make a note of the individual's name. Do not just leave a telephone message on an answerphone or with a clerk or assistant. Give your reasons for concern and make clear if you believe the situation requires immediate response or emergency intervention. State whether the parents have been told of your referral
- record date and time of the referral, details of the conversation, name and post of the individual to whom the referral was made, and their response. Verbal referrals should always be confirmed in writing.

Social services have a legal duty under the Children Act to respond to all referrals where there is concern about a child's well-being. However, informing other professionals of your concerns does not mean you no longer have professional responsibility for the child.

Referrals to social services will be passed to a duty social worker or to a member of the specialist child protection investigation team. A social worker will then visit the family and make an initial assessment of the situation. This should be carried out within 24 hours of the original referral.

Following the initial investigation the social worker will decide, in consultation with their team manager:

- whether a medical examination is needed
- whether legal proceedings should be taken to safeguard the child or to enable the child to be examined by a registered medical practitioner
- whether to call a child protection conference.

The social worker may decide to take no further action following the initial investigation and discussion with their senior manager. In this case they should inform the person who made the original referral and give their reasons. But this may not always happen. If no feed-back has been received within two days of a referral, you should contact the social services department to check that the referral has been acted on.

If social services are not prepared to accept a referral, nor to take action following the initial investigation, and you remain concerned, you should discuss the situation with your child protection adviser or senior nurse manager with child protection responsibilities. She may agree with you that the matter should be pursued further with the social services team manager.

It is possible for any agency or professional to request a child protection conference, and this course of action is open to you if you believe it is necessary. However social services officers remain responsible for organising the case conference.[6]

4.2 **Emergencies**

All social service departments operate an emergency out-of-hours service. If, for whatever reason, you are unable to contact the duty social worker and you consider the situation to be an emergency, you should contact either the local police or the NSPCC. Both these agencies have statutory powers to intervene in situations where a child is at risk of harm, and to remove a child at risk to a place of safety.

4.2.1 **The police**

Contact your local police station. A uniformed officer will attend immediately and, if necessary, remove the child under a police protection order (PPO). The police protection order allows the police to remove the child to a place of safety for up to 72 hours. The police will contact social services, who will arrange accommodation for the child and will follow the usual child protection procedures.

Where criminal proceedings are involved, the case will also be referred to the local police child protection team, or to a designated officer experienced in working with children.

4.2.2 **The NSPCC**

The NSPCC runs a 24-hour national helpline, staffed by trained counsellors. The helpline is free. The counsellor will talk through the situation with the caller, assess the risk to the child and, where appropriate, make an immediate referral either to the nearest NSPCC child protection team or to the local social services. The NSPCC operates 85 specialist child protection teams and projects in England, Wales and Northern Ireland.

NSPCC child protection helpline ℡ 0800 800 500

5 Child protection procedures

All participants invited to attend a child protection conference have the right to make their contribution and to give their professional assessment of the situation. Challenge other people's views if you do not agree with them – and don't be afraid to change your mind after hearing other people's contributions.

Every local authority is required to have in place agreed procedures for instigating and co-ordinating inter-agency child protection procedures. This work will be carried out by the area child protection committee (ACPC).

5.1 The area child protection committee

Membership of the ACPC will include senior representatives from all those agencies likely to be concerned with child protection: social services, health authorities and trusts, education authorities, police and probation services, and local authority legal advisers. Community nurses will be represented on the committee by the trust/health authority senior manager with responsibility for community services and/or the child protection adviser.

ACPC membership may also include the housing department and other statutory and voluntary agencies, if relevant. The committee will be chaired by a senior social services officer.

The role of the ACPC is to ensure effective inter-agency working to protect children. The ACPC is responsible for monitoring inter-agency service provision, and for drawing up local inter-agency child protection policies and procedures, which should be reviewed annually.

Other responsibilities of the ACPC include:
- monitoring use of legal proceedings
- identifying significant issues arising from child protection cases and inquiries

- ensuring that resources are available for work related to child protection
- identifying gaps in provision of services
- initiating and evaluating progress on preventive work
- ensuring inter-agency training is provided
- setting up case management reviews when a child has died through non-accidental injury, or in particularly complex cases of non-accidental injury
- publishing an annual report on local child protection matters.[6]

The ACPC meets between four and six times a year but much of its actual business is carried out through sub-committees with specific responsibility for the key areas of work. These are policy and procedure; monitoring and evaluation; prevention, and training.

All health visitors, school nurses and community nurses should know who represents them on the ACPC and how to contact them.

5.2 **The child protection register**

The child protection register is a central register maintained by every social services department of the names of children in their area who have suffered or are at risk of significant harm. The decision to register a child's name can only be taken at a child protection conference.

The child protection register is a confidential document. Members of the public have no right of access to it. A nominated social services official acts as 'custodian' of the register. Health, medical and other professionals whose concern with a child's health and well-being requires that they know if his or her name is on the register can apply to the custodian for access.

The purpose of the register is:
- to provide a central record, available to the relevant agencies, of all children in the area who are deemed at risk of or known to have suffered significant harm
- to record the category under which a child's name has been registered and the names of the professionals concerned
- to collect accurate, up-to-date statistical information

- to monitor registrations and ensure that registration criteria are being applied consistently.

The ACPC is responsible for producing regular reports (usually every three months) of numbers of entries and removals from the register, numbers under each category for registration, and ethnic origin and age breakdown of children registered.

5.3 **Criteria for registration**

A child's name can only be entered on the child protection register if it is agreed by a child protection conference that:
- she or he is likely to suffer significant harm, or
- she or he has suffered significant harm from one or more identifiable incidents in the following categories:
- **neglect**
  persistent or severe neglect of a child, or failure to protect a child from exposure to danger, including cold or starvation; extreme failure to carry out important aspects of care, resulting in the significant impairment of child's health or development, including non-organic failure to thrive
- **physical injury**
  actual or likely physical injury to a child, or failure to prevent physical injury (or suffering) to a child including deliberate poisoning, suffocation and Munchausen's syndrome by proxy
- **sexual abuse**
  actual or likely sexual exploitation of a child or adolescent
- **emotional abuse**
  persistent or severe emotional ill-treatment or rejection affecting or deemed likely to affect the child's emotional and behavioural development.

A child's name may be entered under more than one registration category but this is not usual practice; multiple registrations are discouraged.[6]

5.3.1 **Significant harm**

'Significant harm' is defined as ill-treatment or the impairment of a child's health or development where:[7]
- the child's health and development is other than that which

could be reasonably be expected of a similar child
- the care given by the parents is not what could reasonably be expected for that child.

Under the Children Act a parent unable to provide a 'reasonable' standard of care is required to seek professional help.

5.4 **The child protection conference**

The child protection conference (CPC) is central to child protection procedures. The prime function of the CPC is to decide if a child's situation meets the criteria for registration on the child protection register, to ensure that a protection plan is implemented and monitored, and to review the need for registration.

It is not the function of the CPC to decide whether an individual has abused a child; that is a matter for the courts.

The child protection conference provides a forum for parents and the professionals concerned with the welfare of the child to discuss the situation and decide:

- whether the child is suffering or is at risk of significant harm, and if so
- whether the child's name should be entered on the register, and if so
- allocation of the case to a key worker.[6]

The child protection conference may also need to decide the likely risk of harm to siblings or other children living in the same household as the child whose situation is causing concern. Their names may also be entered on the register and included in the child protection plan.

A child protection conference can only be convened by social services or by the NSPCC although, as stated above, other professionals may request that it is held. The conference is chaired by a senior social services officer, who has the casting vote in situations where consensus cannot be reached between agency representatives on whether the child's name should be entered on the register.

Only those professionals working directly with the child and family concerned, and with a relevant contribution to make to the conference, should be invited to attend. They may include:

- social worker and social services team manager
- officer from the police child protection team
- NSPCC child protection officer
- head teacher or named member of teaching staff with child protection responsibilities
- health visitor/school nurse/community nurse and child protection adviser/senior nurse
- general practitioner
- day nursery worker
- probation officer.

Some ACPCs have a recommended minimum quorum for child protection conferences, so that decisions about the future care and protection of the child can only be made if representatives from an agreed number of the ACPC member agencies are present at the conference.

It is now established practice in many areas for parents to attend child protection conferences, although there is no legal obligation to include them. Generally it is regarded as good practice to invite the parents to attend at least part of the conference. Parents may feel more confident about attending and more able to speak if they are accompanied by a friend or supporter, and this should be encouraged. However it would not be appropriate for the family's health visitor to act in this capacity, as this would compromise her professional objectivity.

Children deemed of sufficient age and understanding may be invited to attend, and to bring a supporter. Again, this is not routine; the decision will made on an individual basis by the social worker responsible for carrying out the initial assessment, in consultation with the CPC chair.

Parents or carers may be excluded on an individual basis because of risk of violence or disruption, but the likely prosecution of a parent for abuse of the child is not regarded as a justifiable reason for exclusion.[6] They may also be asked to leave temporarily while the final decisions are made on the risk of harm to the child and need for registration.

Including parents in case conferences is in keeping with the principle of partnership with parents established under the

Children Act 1989.[7] It has a number of advantages for the child and parents and for professionals:

- parents are likely to know more than anyone else present about their child and their own situations
- parents have continued responsibility for the child and should therefore share in decisions about the child's future
- professionals will be prompted to keep their contributions accurate, comprehensible and unbiased
- parents will understand the situation better, making it easier for the professionals involved to work with them
- opportunities for misunderstandings and misinterpretations should be reduced if parents hear for themselves what is said.

A child protection conference can be a very intimidating experience for parents. If their attendance is to be of any benefit, the conference chair should arrange for them to be both prepared for and debriefed after the child protection conference.

Details of the conference decisions and minutes of the proceedings should be made available to everyone attending the conference, including the parents. If parents do not attend they must be informed of the decisions, verbally and in writing. This is the responsibility of the conference chair.

An initial child protection conference will be called following the preliminary investigation by social services of an incident or suspected incident of child abuse. It should take place within eight to 15 working days of the original referral, when the initial investigation has been completed and provided all the necessary information is available to the conference.

A review child protection conference will be arranged between three and six months after the child's name has been entered on the register. The purpose of the review conference is to monitor the implementation of the child protection plan and assess the continued need for the child's name to be on the register. Review conferences should be re-convened every six months at least, until the decision is made to remove the child's name from the register.

The decision to remove a child's name from the register will be taken by the child protection review conference. A child's

name will be removed from the register if the majority of those professionals attending the review conference decide that:
- the child is no longer at risk of significant harm, or
- the child and family have moved permanently to another area, or
- the child reaches the age of 18.

A child's name will also be removed from the register in the event of that child's death.

If not invited to attend the review conference, parents and child should be informed in writing of any decisions made.

5.5 **Preparing for the child protection conference**

If you are invited to participate in a child protection conference you will be expected to prepare a written report prior to attendance. The report should describe your professional concerns about the family and child as well as your professional assessment of the family's strengths and capabilities. You should inform your child protection adviser that you have been asked to attend the conference. You may find it helpful to discuss the report with her.

Copies of the report, typed, should be available to all members at the child protection conference, and for inclusion in the conference minutes and the social work file which will be kept on the child and family.

It is good practice to discuss your report with the parents and give them a copy prior to the child protection conference taking place. Parents have a right to know what you are going to say about them at the conference, and to have the opportunity to discuss with you your professional opinion of their situation and the recommendations you intend to make to the conference. Nothing should be included in the report that you do not feel able to say directly to the parents and which you have not already discussed with them.

Parents should be encouraged and helped to present their own views to the conference if they disagree with any of your conclusions. You may, for example, suggest that the parents write their own presentation for distribution at the child protection conference, and help them do so. You may, with their agreement, include their comments in your own report to the conference.

Your report would normally include information on:
- the child's growth and development
- the child's behaviour
- the child's physical and emotional care
- the child's attendance or failure to attend clinic, school, day nursery, GP surgery etc;

your professional assessment of:
- parenting skills
- parent/child interaction
- strengths of family
- future risk to child, and
- your recommendations for action.

You should distinguish clearly between what is factual information and what is your professional opinion, and be able to substantiate your comments.

You may wish your child protection adviser, nurse manager or an experienced colleague to attend the conference with you, to give professional support.

5.6 **Conference procedure**

Every individual invited to attend a child protection conference has the right to make their contribution and give their point of view. It is the job of the conference chair to ensure that each participant is able to speak and contribute equally to the decision-making process.[6]

Don't be afraid to challenge other people's views and opinions if you do not agree with them, or to change your mind after hearing other people's contributions. But:
- keep your contributions short and to the point
- don't interrupt others, and don't let anyone else interrupt you
- keep your contributions relevant.

Ask the chair for a chance to speak if you feel you are being overlooked. If you disagree with a decision, say so at the time; don't wait until the last minute before speaking up. Ask for clarification if there's anything you have not understood.

You should keep your own record of any decisions or recommendations agreed by the conference. This will be useful for future reference should there be a delay in distributing the minutes to the participants.

Don't feel compelled to agree with a majority decision. If you disagree with any issue or decision, make sure this is recorded in the minutes. Situations are rarely cut-and-dried; the fact that not every participant agreed on an issue will give a more realistic picture of a highly complex situation. It is also important that the minutes are completely accurate; the fact that not every professional present could agree to a decision or recommendation may prove important at a later date.

A copy of the minutes of the conference should be sent to all professionals invited to attend, not simply those who attended. Check them carefully to ensure they are an accurate record of the conference. If you need to make any corrections, make sure you send your comments to the conference chair within ten working days of receiving the minutes. The revised, corrected minutes should then be re-circulated.

The minutes are confidential to the participants at the child protection conference and should be kept with your own professional records. They should not be photocopied or passed to a third party without the consent of all the agencies represented at the case conference.

In some areas parents are given a copy of the final minutes. If this is not local practice, parents should be sent written details of the outcome of the conference and of the agreed child protection plan. This is the responsibility of the conference chair.

5.7 Following the child protection conference

If the child protection conference decides to place a child's name on the register, a key worker will be appointed (a social worker) to carry out a more detailed assessment of the child's and family's situation and to draw up a child protection plan, in consultation with the other professionals concerned.

The key worker is responsible for co-ordinating and monitoring implementation of the child protection plan, although they may not be the professional subsequently to have most contact with the family.

The key worker is also responsible for contacting the local authority legal department to instigate any legal action required, either to gain access to the child or to safeguard her safety.

Parents have the right of appeal against the decision to place a child's name on the child protection register. The process for appeal will be detailed in the local ACPC guidelines. You should know this procedure; parents may be unaware that they have this right and may need the process explained to them.

The social services department will also have a formal complaints procedure whereby parents can challenge the actions of social services officers. Here again parents may need professional guidance and support.

A decision not to register a child's name should not mean automatic withdrawal of all social services support. The child and family may still be allocated to a social worker; the child may come under the Children Act definition of 'in need', entitling the family to local authority childcare and support services. A decision not to register a child is by no means the end of the story. Parents whose borderline situation led to the original referral are possibly more likely than most to need and benefit from more intensive professional support and provision of services.

5.8 **The child protection plan**

The main purpose of the child protection plan is to ensure the child's needs for care and safety are met and that her physical and mental well-being are protected. The plan will also include measures to help the parents care appropriately for their child.

Outline recommendations for the child protection plan will be agreed at the first child protection conference. However in most cases more time will be needed to discuss the child and family situation, and for more detailed preparation and planning for the child's care. In this case a separate meeting will be called as soon as possible after the initial child protection conference, to agree a full plan.

Co-ordination of the child protection plan is the responsibility of the key worker. However you will be individually responsible for implementing the parts of the plan which specifically relate to your remit.

5.9 **Supporting parents**

It is important that health and social services maintain contact with parents throughout the child protection process, whether or not the decision is taken to place their child's name on the child protection register. Support should also be available and should continue where a child protection conference decides not to register the child or to remove the child's name from the register. Going through a social services investigation is a traumatic experience. Parents should be informed of appropriate sources of statutory and voluntary support and be made aware of their rights. This is an area where the health visitor's support may be more welcome than that of a social worker or other professional with statutory powers. However parents may wish to have no further contact with the particular professionals involved in the procedure and this should be respected. There are a number of independent agencies which provide counselling and support to parents. These include:

Parents Against Injustice (PAIN)
11 Riverside Business Park
Stansted
Essex CM24 8PL
☏ 0279 647 171

Family Rights Group
The Print House
18 Ashwin Street
London E8 3DL
☏ 071 249 0008 (advice line)
☏ 071 923 2628 (office)

Children's Legal Centre
20 Compton Terrace
London N1 2UN
☏ 071 359 6251

Rights of Women (ROW)
52-54 Featherstone Street
London EC1
☏ 071 251 6577

National Council for One-Parent Families
255 Kentish Town Road
London NW5 2LX
☏ 071 267 1361

6 Court orders and care proceedings

Legal orders should be used sparingly, and only where there is serious concern for the well-being of the child and all efforts to persuade the parents to co-operate have failed.

The Children Act 1989 introduced two orders to enable professionals to obtain access to a child should the parents or carers refuse. These orders are used when a professional believes it is necessary to carry out an assessment of a child's physical and emotional well-being and considers the child may be at risk of significant harm. The orders are:
- the emergency protection order
- the child assessment order.

These orders can be heard by a magistrate alone and need not come before a full family proceedings court.

Two further orders exist for the ongoing care and supervision of the child at risk of significant harm:
- the care order
- the supervision order.

These orders must be heard in a magistrate's court – the family proceedings court – and may be referred to a county court, or even high court if the case is particularly complex or urgent action is required.

6.1 Emergency protection order

An emergency protection order applies where a child is thought to be in immediate danger of suffering significant harm or abuse if action is not taken to protect her. The purpose of the order is to enable statutory authorities to take immediate steps to intervene to protect a child in an emergency.

The emergency protection order replaces the old 'place of safety order'. It is a short term measure, which allows the child to be removed from her current place of residence for a maximum initial period of eight days, and a once-only extension of a further seven days. It can also be used to prevent a child being removed from a place considered safe for her.

Any individual can apply to a magistrate for an emergency protection order, although the most likely authorities will be the social services department, NSPCC or police.

To grant the order the magistrate must be satisfied that:
- the child would suffer significant harm if he were not either removed to alternative accommodation or action taken to prevent his removal, or
- the social services department or NSPCC needs the order to enable them to carry out or continue an investigation into the well-being of a child where there are immediate concerns for the child's safety, or
- an individual believes that a child is suffering or likely to suffer significant harm, that urgent intervention is necessary, but access to confirm this is not possible without a court order.

It is rare for a health visitor, school nurse or other community nurse working with children to be involved in a direct application for an emergency protection order. Normally you will have referred the case to social services, NSPCC or police. You should always seek the professional advice of your child protection adviser, if at all possible, before taking any action through the court process.

A magistrate may grant an emergency protection order with the stipulation that the applicant is accompanied by a registered nurse or health visitor when carrying out the order.

Involvement in a situation where a child is being removed from the family can be stressful and distressing for all concerned. Counselling and support should be available to you. It is the responsibility of your child protection adviser and your manager to ensure this support is provided.[9]

6.2 Child assessment order

The child assessment order is intended for use in situations where there are concerns about a child's well-being but the situation is not thought to require emergency intervention.

The primary purpose of the child assessment order is to allow the statutory authorities access to the child so that an assessment of the child's emotional, physical and social wellbeing can be made.

Only social services and the NSPCC can apply to a court for a child assessment order. For the magistrate to grant the order she or he must be satisfied that:

- there are good reasons to suspect that a child is suffering, or at risk of, significant harm, although not in immediate danger
- an assessment (medical, psychiatric, social work or other) is needed but the parents refuse to co-operate
- all reasonable steps have been taken to persuade the parents to co-operate and these have been rejected.

The order lasts for seven days and requires the parents to allow named professionals access to the child so that the assessments can take place. The order will also specify the kind, place and purpose of the assessments.

You may be the first to identify an unmet health need or possible risk of significant harm to a child. You may feel an assessment is needed because you believe:

- the child appears to be failing to thrive
- the parents are genuinely unaware of or unwilling to accept that their child's safety, health or development is not of an acceptable level
- while not in immediate, serious danger, the child is suffering deliberate neglect and/or abuse
- an assessment would help establish basic facts about a child's condition or situation.

The decision to apply for a child assessment order will usually be taken at a child protection conference. You are likely to be asked to contribute your professional opinion of the child's health and family situation.

The child assessment order should be used sparingly[7] and should only be applied for where there is serious concern about the child, and where all efforts to persuade parents to agree to a voluntary assessment have failed. As the family's health visitor or school nurse, or the nurse they see regularly at the GP surgery, you may have established a relationship of some trust with the parents and may be the appropriate professional to attempt to convince the parents of the need for them to agree voluntarily to their child's assessment.

It is important that the parents are informed that a court order will be applied for if they persist in refusing to co-operate. The court procedure and what the order means should also be explained.

The child assessment order should not be used simply because a parent has refused to use the routine child health services.[7] Parents may agree to a GP or independent health professional carrying out the assessment, and this is an option which should be explained to them.

If you believe that a child assessment order may be needed, you should contact the area social services department or the NSPCC. Whether or not you are the initiator, you are likely to be asked to contribute to the application for an order.

For example:
- a court may request details of your grounds for concern
- a court may seek your 'expert advice' as a health visitor or school nurse about the kind of assessment needed.

Accurate, up-to-date records are vital.

Children deemed capable of understanding the implications of their actions have the right to refuse to comply with a court order for an assessment or other examination.

6.3 Care order

This is a court order which places the child in the care of the local authority. The child may remain at home with her family, or extended family, be placed in local authority accommodation, or be placed with foster parents with a view to adoption.

For a family proceedings court to grant a care order, the judge must be satisfied that the child is or is likely to suffer significant harm because of inadequate parental care, or that the child is beyond parental control.

Under the care order parental responsibility is shared between the local authority and the parent, but the local authority has the final say in deciding the extent to which the parent can exercise this responsibility.

Where a child placed under a care order continues to live at home, or with their extended family, the order will be granted for a specified length of time: usually one to two years. The time limit ensures that the court will be given the opportunity to review the child's situation. The court may decide to allow the order to lapse at the end of the period, if there is no further likelihood of significant harm occurring to the child. Alternatively, the care order may be renewed for a further period, or renewed with a recommendation that the child does not return to their birth family.

Where a child is fostered or otherwise placed away from their birth family, the care order will usually last until the child is formally adopted or reaches the age of 18.

6.4 **Supervision order**

A supervision order places the child under the supervision of the local authority or probation service, and requires the parents to co-operate with the supervising agency. The order states the steps the parents are required to take to ensure the child is no longer at risk of significant harm.

The supervision order is granted under similar, stringent conditions to the care order. It lasts initially for a year, but can be renewed by the court for a maximum of up to three years.

Courts also have powers to grant an interim care order or interim supervision order. Interim orders are similar to full orders but have a restricted duration and can be obtained more easily: where there are 'reasonable grounds for believing' a child is suffering or at risk of significant harm.

6.5 **Further orders**

Other court orders relating to child protection include:
private law orders

- the family assistance order, enabling a court to direct a social services department to provide assistance to a family involved in court proceedings

section eight orders
- the residence order, stating with whom the child is to live and giving that person parental responsibility for the child. This would be the means whereby a father who is not married to the mother of a child obtains parental responsibility for the child
- the contact order, allowing contact between the child and the individual named in the order. This is often used when a child is in the care of a local authority or in divorce proceedings
- the prohibited steps order, preventing the child's parents or other individuals carrying out certain actions in relation to the child without the court's permission
- the specific issue order, covering the handling of specified issues in relation to the child.

7 Court proceedings

The purpose of appearing as a witness is to provide to the court the information it needs to make a decision in the best interests of the child. You are there as an impartial witness, not to take one or other side.

The Children Act 1989 introduced a new form of court, the family proceedings court, specifically to hear cases concerning the care and well-being of children. This is a magistrate's court, and it is here that the majority of cases concerning child protection are heard, although more complex or urgent cases will still be heard in the county court or high court.

Magistrates and judges serving in family proceedings courts receive special training in the Children Act.

Where a local authority is seeking a care or supervision order for a child, or where the interests or wishes of the child and its parents may conflict, the court will appoint a guardian *ad litem* to represent the child's interests to the court. This is likely to be an independent senior social worker. The guardian *ad litem* has powers to arrange for a solicitor to act for the child. Their primary role is to provide a link between the child, the court and the various agencies involved. The guardian *ad litem* has right of access to social services records, but only to those parts of the health records included in them; not to the child health records or the records held by the health professionals themselves.

However you may provide confidential information from your professional records about a child and its family situation if it is in the interests of the child (see page 67). This information may be provided either verbally to the person inquiring or in a written report. In either case you should seek the advice of your child protection adviser or senior nurse manager.

The emphasis in the family proceedings court is to process all cases as quickly and effectively as possible, with the minimum need for court appearances. The Children Act recommends that court proceedings should take no more than 12-16 weeks.[7]

7.1 **Court statements**

If you are required to give evidence in court, you will be asked to submit a written statement of evidence to the court prior to the hearing. This statement will be based on your records relating to your involvement in the child's care, but only those made at the time of the observation. You may also be asked to contribute to the statements of other professionals, usually a social worker or a child's appointed guardian *ad litem*.

Requests for written statements to go before a court will usually come from the local authority's solicitor or the parents' solicitor. You should always seek the advice of your child protection adviser and your employer's legal adviser, both when preparing a statement for court proceedings and when contributing a report to the statement of another professional.

Your statement will generally include details of:
- contacts with the child/family, included failed appointments
- growth and development of the child
- parenting skills of parent(s)
- relationships within the family and effects on the child
- your observations and assessment of significant events
- your professional opinion on the health needs of the child, and of its family
- any conclusions and recommendations – which may include your professional opinion on why an order is needed.

7.2 **Appearing in court**

Having submitted your written statement, you are likely to be asked to appear in court to give your evidence and be cross-examined on it.

Prior to the Children Act 1989 it was common practice for a subpoena to be issued to require a health visitor or nurse to attend court. This was to establish clearly her independence from the statutory proceedings being taken against the parents. The Children Act has now established the principle that the child's interests are paramount, which makes a subpoena no longer necessary or appropriate. A subpoena would only be needed now in civil proceedings where, for example, one parent wished to call you to give evidence on their behalf.

7.3 **Preparation**

If asked by any individual or agency to appear as a witness in court, you should inform your child protection adviser or nurse manager, and seek legal advice from your employer's legal adviser on child protection issues. You are entitled to their advice and support, and should request it if necessary.

You may wish to contact your professional organisation or trade union for advice and support.

You will not be required to appear in court to give evidence to support your written statement if it is accepted by the opposing side in the proceedings and included as evidence in the case. In most cases, however, the lawyers representing the parents will wish to test or amplify the evidence you have given in the statement and you will be called as a witness.

7.4 **Court procedure**

Whether the case is heard in a magistrate's court, county court or high court, the same procedure applies. In the magistrate's family proceedings court the case will be heard by three magistrates; in the county or high court by a judge (but not a jury).

The lawyer presenting the case will call their witnesses in the chronological order of their contact with the family or involvement in the event. When called to give evidence you can refer to your records but not to the statement you have already submitted to the court. Your records will also be available to the court for examination. However only those records made at the time of the event or observation (that is, within 24 hours) are considered valid evidence in court.

The presenting lawyer will take you through the evidence as written in your statement. Then the cross-examining lawyer will ask you questions to test and amplify your statement.

When giving evidence you should speak slowly and clearly,

addressing your replies to the lawyer asking the questions. Keep your responses factual, brief and to the point. If you do not understand the question, or have not heard it clearly, ask for it to be repeated. Do not attempt to elaborate your answer beyond the question; the lawyer will ask further questions if more information is needed.

The purpose of appearing as witness is to provide to the court the information it needs to make a decision in the best interests of the child. You are there as an impartial witness, not to take any one side.

Once the cross-examination is complete the magistrate or judge may wish to ask questions of their own. The presenting lawyer – the lawyer who first called you as a witness – will then be allowed to question you again, but only to re-cap or emphasise what has already been presented to the court; not to raise new issues.

If you are not familiar with court proceedings you may find it helpful to sit in on another case, in advance of your own court appearance. This can usually be arranged through the local magistrate.

7.5 Follow-up

Following the court hearing and judgement, a debriefing should be arranged for all members of the child protection conference concerned with the child. This should be the responsibility of the key worker and their manager.

If the court places the child under a supervision order (that is, remaining with their birth family) the health visitor or school nurse is likely to continue to be involved with his care. Further meetings will be held with members of the child protection conference to agree a care plan for the ongoing monitoring of the child's well-being and support for the family.

Where the court order places the child in care or with a family other than their birth family, she is likely to be moved to another area and the health visitor or school nurse will no longer be involved, other than to ensure the health records relating to the child are passed on as swiftly as possible.

8 Records and record-keeping

Health records should be accurate, legible, factual and contemporaneous. They should be checked, signed and dated. Above all, health records should be read.

Accurate, up-to-date records are never more vital than in child protection. Child abuse inquiries have repeatedly highlighted poor record-keeping as a contributory factor in situations where a child has been harmed.[13]

Health records should be accurate, legible, indelible, unambiguous and factual. They should distinguish clearly between what is fact and what is the health visitor or nurse's professional opinion. They should be maintained in chronological order and be completed within 24 hours of the contact or incident to which they refer. Records should be checked carefully after writing, signed (not initialled) and dated. They should be stored in an area which is not accessible to the general public, but where other professionals who need them can have ready access. Above all, they should be read.[25]

The health visitor's child health and professional (family) health records should together provide a clear, continuous and in-depth picture of the child and its family situation. The information they contain will be crucial to procedures to protect children at risk of harm. They will provide the basis for your contribution to child protection conferences and for your evidence in court proceedings. They may also be required as evidence by the court and, as stated previously, must therefore be completed within 24 hours of the event to which they refer, or as soon as possible thereafter, or they will not be of use in any legal action over a child protection issue.

8.1 Personal (parent-held) child health records
The principles underpinning the use of personal (parent-held)

child health records[26] are that:

- parents need and have a right to be involved in decisions about the health and welfare of their child
- health visitors and community nurses should work in partnership with parents
- information should be shared with parents
- health visitors and community nurses should strive towards a more honest and open relationship with parents.[26]

Working in partnership with parents requires that both practitioner and parent has equal access to the information which will lead to better care of the child and, in the context of health visiting and school nursing in particular, which will assist the parents' confidence and ability in their parenting skills.[26]

Use of personal and parent-held child health records is implicit within the principles of the Children Act 1989. It is now recognised practice in the NHS community health services.[27]

The principle of partnership applies to all health visitors and nurses working with children and families in the community. The national personal and parent-held child health record has, since September 1993, been extended to cover school-age children.[28]

In the context of child protection, use of the personal parent-held child health record allows parents to:

- read your professional assessment of the situation
- use your professional assessment to change their own behaviour
- if they do not agree with it, challenge your assessment from an informed position
- make a more informed decision on when and where to seek help if they feel unable to care adequately for their child, as required under the Children Act.[7]

The parent-held child health record allows you to:

- give parents the information they need to act in the best interests of their own and their child's well-being
- share with the parents any concerns about the health and welfare of their child (where this does not put the child in further danger or risk jeopardising criminal proceedings)
- challenge parents where their notions of parenting are seen to

be inappropriate to the child's well-being.

For the school nurse the record provides opportunity to:
- promote the child's awareness of her health and health needs
- encourage the child to take responsibility for her health
- help the child choose more healthy lifestyle behaviours
- give the child more control over her health and health care
- encourage her to take responsibility for her health.

Training must be provided to all community nursing staff on the introduction and use of the personal parent-held child health record if these principles are to be of benefit in practice.[26,27]

8.2 **Parallel records**

Every NHS community trust should have an agreed protocol on the use of the personal and parent-held child health record. This should detail any other records deemed necessary for the care and protection of the child.

Official guidance from the NHS management executive[28] states that:
- the personal and parent-held child health record should be used as the principle child health surveillance record by all clinical medical officers and health visitors, for both pre-school and school-age children
- health visitors should continue to keep a separate professional (family) health record
- a common professional record, stored centrally, should be used by all community health staff
- GPs will also keep their own, detailed records relating to the child's health.

8.3 **The health visitor record**

In some trusts or health visiting teams it may be agreed policy to use the personal parent-held child health record as the sole record of the child's health, development and health care.

More usual practice, as recommended by the department of health,[27] is for health visitors also to keep a separate, brief professional record of each child on their caseload, and a full professional family record where there is concern for the welfare and safety of a child.

The health visitor's child health record should not be a detailed duplicate of the parent-held record. Its purpose is to provide the basic information you may need to plan the ongoing care of a child, and to plan your own workload. To be of use, however, it must include:

- background information on the child's health and development
- an accurate, contemporaneous chronology of all contacts with the child
- brief details of your observations and assessments of the child's physical and emotional well-being
- brief details of contacts with and referrals to other professionals and agencies
- brief details of any concerns about the child's health.

The professional (family) health record should provide:

- all information needed to support the planning, implementation and monitoring of a child protection plan
- all information needed by colleagues involved in the case in your absence
- all information required for court proceedings.

It should therefore include:

- your observations and assessment of the parents' ability to care appropriately for their child
- details of and your professional assessment of the family situation and social circumstances
- your contacts with other professionals and agencies to discuss concerns about the family.

No record held separately by the health visitor or nurse should contain information or observations which have not already been shared and discussed with the parents. The function of the separate record is to ensure simply that you have immediate access to the factual information and observations you may need for the care and protection of the child. The principle of partnership with parents applies also to record-keeping; the right of individuals to access to their health records, in principle and by law, should be acknowledged.

School nurses may similarly keep a separate record of particular concerns while using the personal child health record to note details of routine health surveillance checks, medical treatment and immunisation information. Again, practice should be governed by local protocols to prevent unnecessary duplication or loss of vital information.

8.4 **Access to health records**
Under the Access to Health Records Act 1990 and the Data Protection Act 1984 clients and patients have the right of access to any personal health records held by health or medical staff, in both manual and computer format.[29] You may only recommend that access is refused to certain parts of the record if you believe what is recorded may cause harm either to the client or to a third party.[28] Parents have the same legal right to see any records relating to the health of their child.

Personal health records held by professionals should always be stored in secure facilities.

The personal parent-held child health record should be regarded in principle as belonging to the child.[28] By law, however, it remains the legal property of the issuing health authority or trust. Access may be obtained, if necessary, by an affidavit requiring the record to be produced as evidence in court. However few parents or children will refuse to allow access to the record for legitimate purposes.

Any document relating to the care of a patient or client can be required as evidence before a court of law or before the professional conduct committee of the United Kingdom Central Council for Nursing, Midwifery and Health Visiting.[25]

8.5 **Transfer of records**
Health records relating to a child and its family should be transferred to their new health visitor or school nurse as soon as possible following the removal of a family and / or child to a new area. There should also be an established procedure for the handover of the health visitor's child and family health records to the school nurse when the child reaches school age. The child protection adviser or designated senior nurse is responsible for ensu-

ring agreed procedures are in place and for monitoring their implementation.[9]

8.6 Confidentiality

Arrangements for the protection of children from abuse, and in particular the effective working of child protection conferences, require that all the professionals concerned co-operate and share and exchange relevant information.[6] But client and professional confidentiality must be respected; everyone involved in a child protection case must be confident that both verbal and written information is confidential to the participants and will be made available only to those outsiders whose need to know is in the best interests of the child.[25]

There are a number of laws, both civil and public, governing access to health records. Confidentiality is also covered by the UKCC code of professional conduct[30] and by NHS employers' contracts of employment. The purpose of these laws and codes is to protect the individual client or patients; they are not intended to prevent the exchange of information between the various professionals and agencies concerned with the protection of children.[6]

Under public law (the common law duty of care) every health visitor and nurse is required to take whatever steps you believe necessary and which come within your professional competence and remit to care for and protect your clients' wellbeing. This includes sharing information, with or without the permission of the child or child's parents, with other professionals who need access to that information for the purpose of protecting the child.

You will not be held to have breached any law of trust or confidentiality provided you can prove, if necessary before a court of law, that the disclosure of information without the consent of the parents or child was in the child's best interests. The Children Act 1989 makes clear that the child's interests must come first, before those of the parents.[7]

Public law takes precedence over civil law. Only if you are unable to justify your disclosure as in the client's interests, and if the disclosure is proved in court to have caused harm to the client, can you be sued for damages under civil law proceedings. Even here, however, you will not be personally liable for any damages awarded by a court (see page 74).

8.6.1 UKCC code of professional conduct

The UKCC code of professional conduct stipulates that every registered nurse, health visitor and midwife must:

- 'act to promote and safeguard the interests and wellbeing of patients and clients', and
- 'ensure no action or omission on your part...is detrimental to the interests, condition or safety of patients and clients'. It is the professional duty of every registered nurse, health visitor and midwife to share information where it is necessary to safeguard the well-being of the child. It is also your professional duty to keep confidential any information disclosure of which may put the child at risk.

If you disclose information without professional justification and without the child or parents' consent, you may be reported to the UKCC for breach of code of conduct and, following investigation by the UKCC professional conduct committee, struck off the register and unable to practise as a registered nurse, health visitor or midwife.[30]

8.6.2 Employment law

You are also personally bound by your contract of employment to respect the confidentiality of clients. You may risk disciplinary action and dismissal if you are found to have disclosed information without professional justification and without the child or parents' consent.

9 Accountability

Every registered health visitor, nurse and midwife, including those in management or specialist adviser positions, is individually accountable for her actions and standards of professional practice.

Discussion of a case with a senior colleague, professional adviser or manager does not remove or lessen the personal accountability or responsibility of the individual registered nurse or health visitor for her standards of practice in the care of a child.[30]

The UKCC code of professional conduct requires every registered nurse, midwife and health visitor to:
- update and maintain skills, competency and standards of practice
- undertake only those duties for which she is trained and is competent to perform safely.[30]

As stated previously, if it is found that an error or omission on your part led to a child suffering harm, you may be struck off the register and unable to practise as a registered health visitor or nurse. You may also be disciplined or dismissed by your employer, for breach of contract. You may also face dismissal from your post if you are struck off the UKCC register and so unable to practise as a registered health visitor or nurse.

9.1 Employer's liability

You can be sued under civil law by a client if the client believes an error or omission on your part led to him or her suffering loss or harm. You will not be liable personally to pay compensation, however. Your employer (whether health authority, NHS trust or GP) holds vicarious liability for your actions and will therefore be liable for any damages or costs. This is the case even where you are found to have caused the loss or damage through your own professional negligence. NHS employers and GPs are insured against such an eventuality.

Figure 2: Lines of accountability

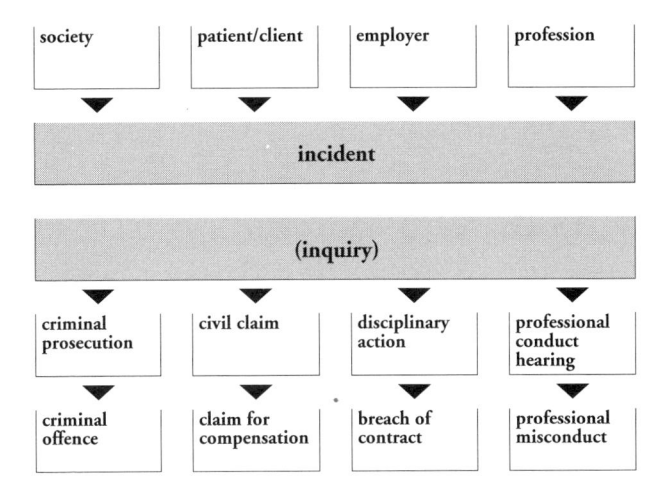

| society | patient/client | employer | profession |

▼ ▼ ▼ ▼

incident

(inquiry)

▼ ▼ ▼ ▼

| criminal prosecution | civil claim | disciplinary action | professional conduct hearing |

▼ ▼ ▼ ▼

| criminal offence | claim for compensation | breach of contract | professional misconduct |

Nor will you be personally liable to pay compensation if the loss or damage is connected with a breach of confidentiality. The health records are the legal property of your employer and it is your employer therefore who is held accountable in law both for any breach of confidentiality and for compensation for any loss or damage caused.

However employer's vicarious liability covers only legal liability for financial compensation. It does not preclude the case coming before the UKCC professional conduct committee and you remain professionally accountable for your individual standard of professional practice.

9.1.1 GP fundholding

Where a health visitor's services have been contracted by a GP fundholder, your employing trust or authority retains vicarious liability for your actions and omissions. However a GP fundholder may be held liable in a court of law if it can be proved that she failed to contract sufficient health visiting time adequately to safeguard the well-being of children registered with the practice.[31]

9.1.2 **Secondment**
Where a health visitor is working on formal secondment to another health authority, trust or other employer, the employer to whom you have been seconded becomes liable for your actions and omissions.

9.2 **Concerns about colleagues**
Your code of professional conduct also includes responsibilities with regard to the professional practice of colleagues. If you believe that a colleague is practising in a way that places the health and safety of clients or colleagues at risk, you are required by the UKCC code of professional conduct to take action.[30]

You should first raise your concerns directly with the colleague, in a non-confrontational and supportive way if possible. If the situation remains unchanged and you are still concerned you should inform your line manager and confirm your concerns in writing. You should also inform your colleague of your actions. You may wish to get advice from your professional association or trade union.

Your manager is obliged, again by the UKCC code of professional conduct, to investigate any reports of concern about the standard of practice of any member of her nursing staff. It is not your responsibility to investigate your concerns, nor to collect evidence from colleagues to support these concerns.

Making a complaint about a colleague's standards of practice is an extremely serious matter, which can lead to disciplinary action, loss of registered status and even dismissal. Your concerns must be well-founded, accurate and relevant, and you must be prepared, if necessary, to stand by them before the UKCC professional conduct committee and before an industrial tribunal.

If you are concerned about the standards of practice of a non-nursing colleague you should follow the same process of first raising your concerns directly with the individual and then reporting the concerns to your line manager. She should then take the matter forward with the appropriate manager.

9.3 **Conflicts of opinion**

Conflicts of opinion will arise between professionals involved in child protection. If you are in a situation where you and a colleague – either within the health service or from another agency or organisation – disagree on an important issue, you should discuss the situation with your child protection adviser or designated senior nurse manager and seek her advice on how to proceed. You may also wish to seek the advice and representation of your professional association or trade union.

10 Prevention

All community nurses play a vital part in the early identification and referral of children at risk of harm. But their unique role, and the role of health visitors in particular, is in providing support for vulnerable families to prevent that harm occurring.

While participation in statutory child protection procedures is an important part of the role of health visitors, school nurses and other nurses working with families and children in the community, it is by no means the whole story.

Health visitors and school nurses in particular have a critical role in strategies to prevent child abuse occurring, both through the early identification of vulnerable children and families and through the support they can offer all families. This role is evident in all three states of preventive intervention.

10.1 Primary prevention

Primary prevention – support for families where actual harm or neglect of a child has not occurred but where there may be a number of risk factors indicating vulnerability – is a key role for community nurses, and for health visitors in particular.

The universal child health surveillance programme is in itself a vital safety net, allowing health visitors to identify potentially vulnerable families and ensure those not previously identified as at risk do not miss out on health and social care. Because the service is universal it avoids the element of social stigma which may be attached to families perceived by the community to have come to the attention of the statutory child protection services.[11,32] Child health clinics have also been shown to be an accessible and popular source of child health care and advice.[33]

Recent years have seen both health visiting and school nursing services develop beyond routine child health surveillance towards targeting more intensive child and family support at those in greatest need.34

Using caseload and community health profiles and, in some cases, specialised 'poverty profiles',35 health visitors and school nurses identify for particular support those families where social, environmental and economic factors take their toll on the parents' ability to care adequately for their child. There are numerous successful examples of such programmes, where health visitors, either individually or as a part of a team, have established ante and post natal support groups, sleep clinics, drop-in centres for single mothers and a wide variety of other family support initiatives.

School nurses may, through their expanding role in health education, take part in classroom teaching on health and sex education and preparation for parenthood. Health and sex education while at school has been shown to encourage more responsible and informed behaviour by children and young people with regard to sexual activity and experimentation.36 Girls and young women who are informed about and feel able to discuss sexual matters are less likely to become pregnant.37 Children and young people may find it easier to talk with a school nurse about personal matters, because she is outside the education system and because of her health expertise.[11,38]

Frequently a health visitor or school nurse will have had contact with a family going back over many years – and over more than one generation. This background knowledge of the family, together with the long-term relationship which has been established, allows the health visitor or school nurse to work more effectively with the parent in developing appropriate care plans, mobilising support from other family members and the wider community, and making appropriate referrals either to other agencies or to self-help and other support groups. Her ability to act autonomously, 'thinking on her feet' and adapting to rapidly changing circumstances and needs, is critical to successful health visiting practice.39

However intervention to improve a family's material circumstances – housing and income (through advice on claiming benefits), for example – can be more acceptable and effective than any amount of advice and counselling to relieve family stress.[40] Here the health visitor and community nurse has a valuable role as advocate, supporting a family's request for a housing transfer, for example.

Traditionally home visiting has been seen as central to the health visitor's role, enabling her to assess the family in its social and environmental context, and to advise parents on safety and other measures to prevent accidental injury or ill-health. Home visits by trained professionals have been shown to be effective in improving parenting skills in high risk families, and consequently the health of their children.[41]

Families in temporary and homeless accommodation risk falling through the health and social welfare support net and the health visitor, through her outreach work in the community, can establish and maintain contact with such highly mobile families. This also means that families deemed at high risk are 'followed' by the statutory health and social services and contact is maintained, especially where a family is not registered with a general practitioner.[42]

Many health visitors are involved in more intensive, specialist home visiting and support schemes, working alongside the traditional health visiting service. One such programme, now operating in many of the more deprived inner cities, is the first-parent visiting scheme: part of the child development programme developed by the Bristol early childhood development unit. This has been shown radically to improve parenting skills by promoting both the parents' confidence in their own ability to cope with, and their enjoyment of, their child.[43,44]

Another similarly intensive intervention shown to be effective with identified vulnerable families is the 'Nurture program': a 15-week therapeutic and educational programme involving health visitors and clinical psychologists.[45,46]

Other projects which aim to support vulnerable parents and their children and improve parenting skills and confidence include multi-agency centres where young, often unsupported mothers can come with their children. These centres offer a range of education and support services, from basic home-management to counselling and assertiveness training.[47]

Access to an adequate income, housing and statutory welfare services, as stated above, is the key to improving a vulnerable-family's situation. Some health visitors work solely in community development projects aimed at improving social, environmental and economic conditions within deprived areas.[48] Such work is part of the health visitor's wider public health remit, and an important aspect of her role.

10.2 **Secondary prevention**

Where a family has been identified as 'high-risk' — where, for example, one child has already been abused or taken into care — the health visitor or school nurse may be a more acceptable source of support to the family than a professional with statutory powers to intervene and remove a child.[11]

Health visitors and school nurses can make an important contribution to the work of multi-agency family centres aiming to support high-risk families and promote better parenting.[49,50]

10.3 **Tertiary prevention**

This describes strategies to safeguard the abused child against further harm and, where the child remains with the family, to promote parenting skills. Health visitors, school nurses and, in some cases, practice nurses, may be involved in the multi-disciplinary child protection plan agreed between the child protection conference and the child's parents to monitor and promote the child's well-being. Health visitors may see the child and parents regularly at clinic, or in their home, to monitor the child's continued physical and emotional well-being. They may also be involved in intensive parent-support programmes for families experiencing problems with parenting, to help the parents cope better with the emotional or practical problems which may have contributed to the abuse.

School nurses may be similarly involved, in collaboration with teaching staff and other members of the school community, in the ongoing assessment of a child's well-being, and in providing support to that child and its family.

Specialist, multi-disciplinary health and welfare programmes have been shown to improve parenting skills and to be of benefit to families deemed to be 'high-risk'.[51,52]

Self-help and voluntary groups also play a critical role in supporting vulnerable families. The health visiting service is not always acceptable or appropriate to the needs of families. In some areas health visitors work in partnership with 'community mothers': another programme from the Bristol EDCU.[53] The community mothers are experienced local mothers who complement with peer group support the more specialist and professional input offered by the health visitor, offering encouragement and one-to-one help that is seen as more acceptable by the families with whom they work.[54] This applies also to families from ethnic minority groups, who will have very particular language and cultural needs.[55]

Other self-help groups exist, frequently with the active support and participation of local health visitors. These include services aimed at families on the brink of crisis, such as Newpin and Homestart.[56,57]

Newpin provides centres where women can receive counselling, peer group support and access to training and education. Its workers are frequently women who themselves have survived similar pressures and difficulties with their children.

Homestart organises teams of volunteer, experienced parents to provide one-to-one support to new parents struggling to cope with their baby.[57]

10.4 Area child protection committees

Finally, all area child protection committees are required[6] to set up sub-committees with a specific remit in prevention. Their responsibilities include the co-ordination of activities aimed at raising public awareness of child abuse; developing training programmes for youth groups, school and voluntary and community organisations; producing resource lists of services available locally to support children at risk and their families, and identifying gaps in local resources and service provision that should be brought to the attention of the ACPC.

>   Newpin
>   Sutherland House
>   Sutherland Square
>   London SE17 3PE
>   ℡ 071 703 5271

>   Homestart
>   2 Salisbury Road
>   Leicester LE1 7QR
>   ℡ 0533 554 988

Conclusion

Protecting children and working with vulnerable families require a high degree of professional skill and experience. Health visitors are key to the identification and assessment of children at risk; school nurses are playing an increasingly important role with older children; other nurses working with children in the community and working in primary health care also form a part of the safety network.

Health visitors and nurses are in close and frequent contact with children and their families. As health professionals, their advice and support is often welcomed where other, statutory services are not acceptable to a family.

Health visitors and school nurses in particular need specialist training in child protection procedures, and all nurses should be given professional support, advice and supervision by specialist advisers and appropriately qualified and experienced senior nurse managers.

Child abuse is still with us; improved inter-agency working has, it is to be hoped, prevented more tragedies occurring. But there is no room for complacency. A society in which young children are subjected to physical, emotional and sexual abuse must also be prepared to invest in professional services to safeguard its most vulnerable members. Qualified health visitors and nurses are part of that investment and their specialist skills, knowledge and expertise, and their contribution to preventive strategies and ongoing support for vulnerable families, cannot be overlooked.

References

1. Department of Health. *Children and young people on child protection registers. Year ending 31 March 1993. England.* London: HMSO, 1994
2. Creighton, S J. *Child abuse trends in England and Wales 1988-1990.* London: NSPCC, 1992
3. National Childrens' Homes. *Deep in debt.* Report. October 1992
4. NSPCC. *Act now for children.* Campaign pack and information. September 1992
5. Labour party survey. *Child protection under threat.* July 1993
6. Home office, Departments of Health and Education and Science, Welsh Office. *Working together under the Children Act 1989: a guide to arrangements for inter-agency co-operation for the protection of children from abuse.* London: HMSO, 1991
7. Department of Health. *The Children Act 1989: an introductory guide for the NHS.* London: HMSO, 1991
8. Health visitors' association. *The Children Act 1989: guidance on professional practice.* London: HVA, 1990
9. Department of Health. *Child protection guidance for senior nurses, midwives and health visitors.* London: HMSO, 1992
10. Health visitors' association. *Principles into practice: an HVA position statement.* London: HVA, October 1992
11. Appleby F. *In pursuit of excellence. Health visitor* 1991; 64, 8: 254-256
12. Roberts J. *Why are some families more vulnerable to child abuse?* In Brown K, Davies C, Stretton P (eds). *Early prediction and prevention of child abuse.* Chichester: John Wiley, 1988
13. Department of Health. *Child abuse: a study of inquiry reports 1980-1989.* London: HMSO, 1991
14. Greenland C. *Preventing child abuse and neglect deaths: an international study.* London: Tavistock, 1987
15. Department of Health. *Diagnosis of child sexual abuse for doctors.* Standing Medical Advisory Committee report. London: HMSO, 1988
16. RCP. *Physical signs of sexual abuse in children.* Report. Royal College of Physicians of London. April 1991
17. Bagley C, King K. *Child sexual abuse: the search for healing.* London: Routledge, 1990
18. Mrazek PB. *Group psychotherapy with sexually abused children.* In Mrazek PB, Kempe CH (eds). *Sexually abused children and their families.* Oxford: Pergamon Press, 1981
19. NSPCC. *Protecting children: a guide for teachers on child abuse.* London: NSPCC, 1989
20. Smith, G. *Sexual abuse training course.* Department of Health / Institute of Child Health
21. Marchant R. *Myths and facts about sexual abuse and children with disabilities. Child abuse review* 1991; 5:2
22. Marchant R, Page M. *Bridging the gap: child protection and children with disabilities.* London: NSPCC, 1993
23. Westcott HL. *Abuse of children and adults with disabilities.* London: NSPCC, 1993
24. *Female circumcision.* Minority Rights Group, 1991
25. UKCC. *Standards for records and record keeping.* UKCC, 1993

26 Health visitors' association. *In their own hands: introducing parent-held child health records.* London: HVA, 1990
27 NHSME. *Personal child health records.* Guidance letter EL(93)86. Leeds: Department of Health. 8 October 1993
28 BPA. *Parent-held and professional records used in child health surveillance.* Report of the first and second joint working parties. London: BPA, 1993
29 Government health departments. *Guide to the Access to Health Records Act 1990: a guide for the NHS.* London: HMSO, 1990
30 UKCC. *Code of professional conduct for nurses, midwives and health visitors.* UKCC, 1992
31 *Guidance on the extension of the hospital and community health services elements of the GP fundholding scheme from 1 April 1993.* Leeds: NHSME, 1993
32 Dingwall R, Robinson K. *Policing the family? Health visiting and the public surveillance of private behaviour.* In Beattie A et al (eds). *Health and well-being: a reader.* Basingstoke: Macmillan, 1993
33 Dworkin P et al. *Maternal perceptions of child health care. Health visitor* 1990; 63, 10: 339-341
34 Oxfordshire health visitor development group. *A change for the better.* Oxfordshire health authority, 1988
35 Blackburn C. *Poverty profiling.* London: HVA, 1991
36 Jones EF et al. *Teenage pregnancy in industrialised countries.* New Haven: Yale University Press, 1986
37 Jones EF et al. *Pregnancy, conception and family planning services in industrialised countries.* New Haven: Yale University Press, 1989
38 Jackson C. *Fighting for the future. Health visitor* 1993; 66, 5: 159-160
39 Cowley S. *Skill mix: value for whom? Health visitor* 1993; 66, 5: 166-168
40 Goodwin S. *Breaking the links between social deprivation and poor child health. Health visitor* 1991; 64, 11: 376-380
41 Weiss HB, Jacobs FH (eds). *Evaluating family programs.* New York: Aldine de Gruyter, 1988
42 HVA/GMSC. *Homeless families and their health.* London: BMA, 1989
43 Early Childhood Development Unit. *Child protection: the impact of the child development programme.* Bristol: ECDU, 1992
44 Barker W, Anderson R. *The child development programme: an evaluation of process and outcomes.* Bristol: ECDU, 1988
45 Bavolek SJ, Comstock CM, McLaughlin JA. *The Nurturing program: a validated approach for reducing dysfunctional family interactions.* Final report: project number 1RO1MH34862. Rockville: National Institute of Mental Health, 1983
46 Bavolek SJ, Comstock CM. *The Nurturing program: a validated approach for reducing dysfunctional interactions among abusive families. International Child Resource Institute,* 1984; 2: 6-24
47 Billingham K. *Working in partnership with parents. Health visitor* 1989; 62, 5: 156-157
48 Boyd M et al. *The public health post at Strelley.* Nottingham: Strelley nurse development unit, 1993
49 Polnay L. *A service for problem families. Archives of Disease in Childhood* 1985; 60, 9: 887-890
50 Hayes E. *Learning to be good parents. Nursery World* 29 June 1989
51 Armstrong KA. *A treatment and education program for parents and children who are at risk of abuse and neglect. Child abuse and neglect* 1986; 5: 167-175
52 Berkeley Planning Associates. *Exploration of client characteristics, services and outcome: evaluation of the clinical demonstration of child abuse and neglect.* Berkeley: BPA, 1982

53 Johnson Z, Howell F, Molloy B. *Community mothers programme: a randomised, controlled trial of non-professional intervention in parenting. British Medical Journal* 1993; 306, 6890: 1449-1452

54 Suppiah C. *Working in partnership: health visitors and community mothers. Health visitor* 1994; 67, 2: 51-53

55 Jackson C. *Community mothers: trick or treat? Health visitor* 1992; 65, 6: 199-201

56 Pound A. *NEWPIN and child abuse. Child abuse review* 1991; 5, 1: 7-10

57 Harrison M. *Working with young families in their homes. Adoption and Fostering* 1982; 6, 3: 15-18

Appendix 1:
Family Rights Group child protection plan agreement

For children who are not in local authority accommodation or care.
Each participant should be given a copy of the completed agreement.

Child's name

Date of birth

Religion

Ethnicity

First language

1	This should include parents, the key worker and others who are directly involved in work to protect the child. Every attempt should be made to enable children (where old enough) to be participants in this agreement	Names and roles of participants to agreement
2	What led to registration of the child's name on the child protection register? These should be specific and identify conditions and/or behaviours – these should be additional to a careful note of the decisions of a conference (preferably by all participants to this agreement receiving conference minutes). Describe the problems in simple and clear terms. Note if different participants have different opinions	Problems ie. what is now wrong
3	What objectives will everyone work towards? They must be ones that the participants agree can be achieved where progress can be measured. Keep them simple and clear and give a priority to them. Tasks to reach the objectives are detailed below	Objectives ie. what is needed

4	When are these objectives to be achieved?	Time limit
5	Brief details of who, what, when and why are needed here. Check to see if there is an order of priority for doing the work outlined here, and check to see that no one thinks there are any particular obstacles in the way of completing it. As before, keep things simple and clear	Work to be done ie. who will do what to achieve the objectives. **a** by the key worker **b** by the main worker with the family (if different from key worker) **c** by the parents **d** by the child (if involved in agreement) **e** by workers in the core group (this will have to be agreed with them later if they are not present at this meeting) **f** by others
6	Who will visit whom, when and why? • key worker • other participants to the agreement	Frequency and purpose of social work and other agency contact with family and child
7	When will progress towards the objectives be reviewed? Will there be a number of reviews before the time limit noted in above? Will this take place during a child protection review conference? If not, how will it fit with that conference?	Review of progress
8	What are the means of dealing with any dissatisfactions of any participant, or for changing this agreement? What is the appeal procedure?	Dissatisfactions and changes
9	What are the plans for the child if the objectives are not achievable? Give a broad indication of a contingency plan, and/or state clearly that changes to this agreement will not be made before full discussion with at least the participants to this agreement	Contingencies

Prime responsibility for work with the child and the family during this period will rest with:

Name

Workplace address

☎

List the participants to the making of this agreement, with a note of any dissentions and by whom:

Names   Signatures

Date

© FRG and NFCA

Further copies of this agreement may be obtained from:

Family Rights Group
The Print House
18 Ashwin Street
London E8 3DL
☎ 071 923 2628

National Foster Care Association
Francis House
Francis Street
London SW1P 1DF
☎ 071 828 6266

Appendix 2:
Child summary sheet

Health visitor school nurse
Summary of case conference / removal in and out

Name of family _____   Conference review date [   ]

Name of child _____   Date of birth [   ]

| Developmental progress | Normal [ ] | Delayed [ ] | Impaired [ ] |

Physical growth   Centile height [   ]   Centile weight [   ]
                  Date [   ]   Date [   ]

Projected centile height [   ]   Not known [   ]

	Good	Adequate	Poor
Physical care	[ ]	[ ]	[ ]
Nutrition	[ ]	[ ]	[ ]
Emotional care	[ ]	[ ]	[ ]

Behaviour   Normal [ ]   Cause for concern [ ]

Attendance at clinic or school medical examinations   Adequate [ ]   Failed appointments [ ]

Immunisation uptake   Good [ ]   Delayed [ ]   Declined [ ]

	Yes	No
Professional worries about child's school attendance	[ ]	[ ]
Hospital visits	[ ]	[ ]
Hospital admission/s	[ ]	[ ]
Cause for concern incidents	[ ]	[ ]
Cause for concern incidents discussed with parents	[ ]	[ ]

Reproduced with permission from the Royal London Trust

Appendix 3:
Child protection summary sheet

Name of family

Address

_____

_____

_____

Significant harm
Reflected in child's behaviour, growth, development, condition

_____

_____

_____

_____

_____

_____

Aspects of parenting
Parental behaviours (omissions, commissions) that have caused harm or are likely to cause harm

_____

_____

_____

_____

_____

_____

Reproduced with permission from the Royal London Trust